Wineries of Michigan

A Guide to the Wineries and Vineyards of Michigan

By D. L. Tadevich

PUBLISHING-PLUS

Publishing Plus:
A division of Insurance Publishing Plus Corporation
11690 Technology Drive
Carmel IN 46032 USA

Acknowledgements

I would like to thank all of those who participated in helping to create this guide. My special thanks go to Walter J. Gdowski, chairman and CEO of Insurance Publishing Plus, without whom this book would not have been published. I would also like to thank the Michigan Grape and Wine Industry Council for their valuable input. And finally, a special acknowledgment goes to my two daughters, Isabella and Melanie, who were my greatest and most enthusiastic supporters.

Wineries of Michigan

A Guide to the Wineries and Vineyards of Michigan

By D. L. Tadevich

Writer
D. L. Tadevich

Project Editor
Heidi Newman, Mark My Word!
Indianapolis, Indiana

Designer
Karen J. Kennedy, Major Productions, Inc.
Indianapolis, Indiana

Photographers
Jeff Robbins, Carmel, Indiana

Steve Sadler, Grand Rapids, Michigan

Grape and Winery Photo Art
Cheryl Rogers,
Scappoose, Oregon

First Edition, 2001

p PUBLISHING-PLUS

Publishing Plus:
A division of Insurance Publishing Plus Corporation
11690 Technology Drive
Carmel IN 46032 USA
(800) 211-3257

ISBN 0-9704154-1-9

Printed in Canada

Table of Contents

D. L. Tadevich

Author of Wineries of
Indiana, A Guide to the
Wineries and Vineyards
of Indiana. *Tadevich's
education includes a B.A. in English Literature
from the University of Iowa, an M.A. in American History from New York University, and
an archival management and historical editing
certificate from New York University. She
founded Tadevich & Associates in New York
City, a company specializing in photo journal-
ism books and high-tech permanent historical
exhibits. Today she lives in Indianapolis with
her two daughters. Debra has received a Clari-
on Award for popular history writing, and a
New York Festivals International Television
Advertising Award. She is also listed in* Who's
Who in Women in Business.

Michigan is a well-kept secret with beautiful lakeshore drives, winding dirt roads, bed and breakfasts, bistros and sandy beaches galore!! The wine industry is the biggest secret of all, but word is spreading fast. Michigan wineries have blossomed in the last ten years and consequently have tripled their wine production.

Michigan has four designated viticultural areas: Leelanau Peninsula, Lakeshore, Fennville, and Old Mission Peninsula. You might be surprised to discover that Leelanau Peninsula has 211,200 acres of wine grapes and Napa Valley in California is only 7% larger. You might also be surprised to discover that Lake Michigan's shore has an abundant 1,280,000 acres of wine grapes–surpassing Napa Valley's.

Michigan is located ideally for wine grapes, particularly its southwest and northwest. The warm breezes from the lakes and bays extend the growing season and this is ideal for old world grapes: the viniferas such as Chardonnay, Pinot Grigio, Riesling, Cabernet Franc and Pinot Noir. The northernmost of Michigan's wine regions is located on the 45th parallel, the same latitude as the great European regions producing Bordeaux and Chianti wines.

The wineries are set up for tourists and locals alike. You can increase your appreciation of Michigan by visiting the wineries and buying some of the local flavor. You won't be disappointed. Tour, sample, and enjoy Michigan's wineries with me.

Cheers! 🍷

D. L. Tadevich

The Michigan Grape & Wine Industry Council invites you to visit our wineries.

There are so many interesting aspects to wine and wine-making. Grape growing conditions unique to Michigan's climate contribute to the quality and style of the world-class wine you'll enjoy at the winery tasting rooms. During your visits, you'll be captivated by the scenic beauty of the vineyards and hear interesting stories of the proud and dedicated families who devote themselves to their craft. You are sure to come away from each winery visit with a new understanding of the wine industry in Michigan.

If you are not familiar with Michigan wines, the quality may surprise you! Michigan wines continue to set new standards for the future, with more than 500 medals awarded in 12 national and international competitions in 2000. The state is also attracting interest from wine writers around the world as word spreads of the wonderful wines that can be produced in the Great Lakes climate and soil conditions.

Please visit our Web site at www.michiganwines.com to plan your trip to Michigan's wine country. You'll find informative articles, a listing of upcoming events and winery tour maps to guide you through Michigan's spectacular wine regions.

Linda Jones, Program

Manager with The

Michigan Grape & Wine

Industry Council

Winery Openings 2001

Contessa Wine Cellars
Tony Peterson
3235 Friday Road
Coloma, MI 49038
I-94 to Exit 39, south on Friday Road, 1/4 mile
Expected to open - Fall 2001

Lone Oak Vineyard Estate
Kip and Denise Barber
8400 Ann Arbor Road
Grass Lake, MI 49240
I-94 to exit 147 (close to Jackson).
Directly off the exit.
(517) 522-8167
Expected to open - June 30.

David Creighton,

Promotional Specialist with

The Michigan Grape & Wine

Industry Council.

History of Wine Making in Michigan

A Tale Of Two Regions

Michigan's winemaking history spans two centuries. In the period just before the Civil War, disease destroyed America's largest wine-producing region along the Ohio River near Cincinnati. The remnants of that industry migrated to the already recognized grape-growing region along Lake Erie. This area quickly became, in its turn, the leading wine region in the country. By 1880, vineyards extended west and north past Toledo into Southeast Michigan. In 1919, there were eight wineries near Monroe, none of which survived Prohibition.

Southwest Michigan's wine industry fared much better. Also a recognized wine region in 1880, Southwest Michigan received help from an unlikely source. Temperance advocate Dr. Thomas Welch created the first "unfermented wine," as Welch's Grape Juice was originally called, for use in his church's communion service. It quickly caught on with the public. The newly formed Welch's Grape Juice Company encouraged planting of the Concord grapes from which their product was made. The largest of these plantings were in Western New York and Southwest Michigan. By 1900 Concord grapes had become the foundation of Michigan's wine industry as well. The opening of a Welch's plant in Lawton, near Paw Paw, in 1919, helped the area's grape growers survive Prohibition.

A Taste Of The Times

The red-skinned Concord and similar white-skinned Niagara varieties are close relatives of vines native to eastern North America. They are often called by their scientific name – vitis labrusca. Contemporary wine industries are built on Cabernet, Chardonnay, and other fine wine varieties; but at the turn of the century, most American wine was quite different. New York, Ohio, Missouri and Michigan were large wine producers, and nearly all the grapes used were native labrusca varieties. The pungent, usually sweet and often fortified wines made from these grapes were extraordinarily popular. (Even California produced predominantly sweet and fortified wines on into the 1960s!) In the 1940s and 1950s Michigan wineries were so successful at meeting consumer demand, that 80 percent of all wines sold in Michigan were produced in Michigan.

The Times They Are A-Changin'

The 1960s saw many changes come to America, including a change in the kinds of wines we drank. Some claim that soldiers living in Europe adopted the local customs of drinking drier table wines with meals. Some claim increased prosperity and travel contributed to the process. Americans such as Julia Child, Frank Schoonmaker and others certainly added their influence by writing about European foods and wines. By 1968, Americans' tastes had changed enough that, for the first time, consumers purchased more of the drier table wines than the sweeter dessert and fortified wines.

This was a revolution in American culture. And it was a revolution that eastern wineries in general and Michigan wineries in particular were ill suited to accommodate. The grapes that worked so well up until then failed miserably to make the drier table wines to which consumers were flocking. The industry's biggest strength was now its biggest weakness. Of Michigan's highly successful wineries from the 1950s only one has survived: St. Julian. (The St. Julian Wine Company, under the leadership of David Braganini, has actually thrived-becoming the fortieth largest winery in the United States and being named Winery of the Year 1998 by Tasters Guild.)

A New Beginning

In retrospect, this near complete housecleaning of the Michigan wine industry forced us to evolve into a truly fine wine industry with the ability to produce world-class wines. Other eastern wine industries suffered, but none saw the near complete collapse that occurred in Michigan. When our industry was rebuilt, it was rebuilt with the right grapes and the right personnel. The new owners and winemakers were dedicated to producing the finest European- style table wines and planted grape varieties with this in mind.

The modern Michigan wine industry is built upon two major grape types. Hybrid varieties, sometimes called French-American hybrids, produce good quality table wines and are also cold-hardy and disease-resistant. With names like Vignoles and Chambourcin, hybrids deserve to be better known than they are. The other type includes traditional European varieties such as Chardonnay and Merlot. These European varieties are often referred to by their scientific name – vitis vinifera.

In the late 1950s and early 1960s, the first hybrid grape varieties were introduced into Southwest Michigan. The first European varieties were planted around 1970 on Mt. Tabor in Berrien County by Len Olsen and Carl Banholzer. Tabor Hill Vineyard and Winery still produces excellent wines from some of those original vines.

Southwest Michigan continues to produce large amounts of juice grapes – enough to make Michigan the fourth

largest grape-growing state. But this area also produces about half of Michigan's wine grapes. Growers here have found that wine grapes can be extremely profitable, and they are increasingly ready to plant and properly care for the more tender but valuable hybrid and vinifera varieties.

A New Region

In the 1970s, an entirely new wine region was born in northwest lower Michigan near Traverse City. On the Leelanau Peninsula, Bernie Rink planted the first French-American hybrid vines. Larry Mawby, Bruce Simpson and others soon followed. Over on the Old Mission Peninsula, Ed O'Keefe became convinced – contrary to all accepted wisdom – that Riesling and other vinifera varieties could also be grown. He was proven correct. Today, both the Leelanau and Old Mission peninsulas are predominantly vinifera grape regions. Riesling, Chardonnay, Pinot Noir, Merlot, Cabernet Franc, Gewürztraminer, Pinot Gris and Pinot Blanc all vie for attention. And the number of wineries in the area has increased from an original five to over sixteen and continues to grow.

Real Quality

In the past 30 years, Michigan winegrape growers, winery owners, winemakers and other industry associates have revolutionized our wine industry. To meet changing consumer preferences, today's vintners concentrate on finding the best varieties and locations, and utilize the latest technological advances in viticulture and enology. With an impressive dedication to quality, they produce excellent everyday wines as well as an increasing number of world class wines. 🍷

Food and Wine Pairing

By Jill A. Ditmire

A glass of wine is one of life's simple pleasures. Pair that wine with a specific food or dish and simple becomes sublime. And don't get me wrong–a glass of crisp, fruity Michigan Riesling is tasty on its own, but most wine is better when enjoyed with food. Sipping that Riesling with a grilled veal chop smothered in a sauce of morels, scallions, herbs and butter makes one appreciate the incredible layers of flavor in both the wine and the food.

When it comes to pairing wine with food there are no rules, only guidelines, which when followed will enhance your dining experience. But remember the golden rule of wine: drink what you like, when you like, with what you like. If you prefer Chardonnay with a steak, then do it. If someone tells you that's wrong….don't have dinner with them! If you're willing to take your palate to new levels, then see how easy it is to pair the wide variety of tasty Michigan wines with your favorite foods.

There are generally two ways of going about pairing wine with food–complementary or contrasting pairings. Complementary pairing means selecting dishes and wines with similar qualities, be it taste, structure or style. Rich, creamy foods with rich, creamy wines. Wines aged in oak with buttery or smoked foods which echo the nuances oak aging and malolactic fermentation bring to wine. Tart, young wines with hints of spice or racy acidity with highly seasoned cuisines.

Contrasting pairing does what it says, matching a dish with one flavor with a wine that offers an opposite mouth feel. Rich, creamy foods with crisp, tart wines. Sweet, fruity wines with hot, spicy foods.

The guidelines work for both red and white wines. Michigan wines make terrific food partners. And while you will find familiar varietals (Chardonnay, Cabernet Sauvignon, Merlot) we hope you give those that are not so familiar (Scheurebe, Pinot Gris, Vignoles) a try. Michigan wines are terrific with all cuisines and are especially nice with the bounty of foods native to the state–cherries, peaches, morels, game and fish, to name a few. Pair a Michigan wine with a Michigan food product and you too will "Say Yes to Michigan."

The Whites

Chardonnay - Michigan Chardonnay offers a tropical fruit nose and is usually aged in oak which adds layers of buttered, smoky oak and vanilla to the usual tastes of melon and pear. Enjoy with creamy white pasta sauces,

Ditmire is the creator, producer and host of "The Good Life with Jill Ditmire." This is a weekly PBS television show which explores, educates and entertains viewers about wines and foods that are not only from the Midwest, but also from around the world. Jill also contributes regular features on food and wine to Indianapolis Monthly, DINE *magazine and* Indywine.com.

Middle Eastern cuisine (Baba Ganoush, Hummus) lobster with butter sauce, smoked fish, Chicken Piccata.

Chardonel - A French-American hybrid which claims parentage from Chardonnay and Seyval Blanc. You'll find similar qualities of Chardonnay in Chardonel aged in oak: tropical fruit nose, medium-bodied with hints of butterscotch and pear. Enjoy as you would Chardonnay. Chardonel in stainless steel offers more racy acidity, a nose of tropical fruits but medium-bodied flavors of pear, melon, green apple and a hint of lime zest. Pair with grilled fish topped with Michigan fruit chutney, or cheese and green chile quesadillas.

Vignoles - This medium-bodied white can be blended to produce a sweet, semi dry or dry style wine–offering aromas of soft peach and apricot and a touch of fruity sweetness. Semi dry and dry style work well as an aperitif with mild cheeses (Havarti, Port Salut), cream cheese-based dips with crudités, salsas (the sweetness of the fruit cuts the bite of the spice), Cajun cuisine, or Maki rolls (especially those with crab, tuna or avocado). Sweet style is delightful on its own or paired with fresh Michigan peach slices for dessert.

Pinot Gris - Can be found as a light or medium-bodied crisp, smooth still wine with a buttery nose and hints of melon, steel and smoke. When made in a sweet or Tokay style, the wine offers the same aromas and flavors, only intensified. Pinot Gris goes well with shellfish, mild cheese, or grilled fish with a squeeze of lemon. The sweet style IS dessert.

Riesling - Most Michigan Rieslings are bottled to bring forth the fruit–honeysuckle and orange zest– and done in a style which leaves a bit of residual sugar, thus producing not only a fruity wine but a sweet one as well. Enjoy with barbecued beef tenderloin, grilled pork chops with Michigan Cherry Sauce, Onion and Goat Cheese Tartlets. Late Harvest Riesling is an intensely fruity, full-bodied, silky wine that is meant to be dessert or enjoyed with full, rich, flavorful cheese or a wonderful dessert featuring Michigan cherries (Sacher Torte, Bing Cherry Soup).

Gewürztraminer - This medium-bodied white offers both spicy aromas and flavors that make it a perfect food partner for Thai, Indian and Szechwan-style cuisine. Hints of spiced peach, honeysuckle and nutmeg work well with smoked Michigan fish, Biryani Chicken, Lamb Saag and Pad Thai.

Scheurebe, "The lost grape of Germany" - Incredible floral nose of rose petals and lavender. Silky, medium-bodied with lush flavors of pears drizzled with honey, white peach, and a touch of Earl Grey. You'll only find this at Heart of the Vineyard. And if Rick Moersch still has a bottle to sell, let alone taste…don't hesitate. A rare find anywhere in the world–but you just found it in Michigan.

Other Whites

Seyval Blanc - Medium body with hints of melon, pear, and citrus zest. Delicious with cheese (Brie, Gouda, Fontina), seafood (scallops, shrimp, grilled lobster) Indian cuisine (green and red curries, Saag Paneer, Biryani of all types, Tandoori Chicken), or white clam sauce on pasta.

Vidal Blanc - Medium body, dry, crisp, tart– made in the style of a grassy, herbal-tinged Sauvignon Blanc. Great food wine with Michigan fish (sautéed, grilled), any vegetarian dish, (especially Chinese stir-fry), Greek vegetables, anything with morels, and lentil soup.

Cayuga - A native American grape which makes crisp, slightly sweet wine just right for sipping before dinner or served with light fare: cold pasta salads, tuna salad sandwiches, or poached chicken.

Catawba - Another native American grape which produces a wine with a floral nose and almost White Zinfandel-like taste. Serve with fresh fruit, mild cheese (Baby Swiss, Colby).

Niagara - Another native American grape sometimes blended with others or bottled alone to produce an experience that's just like eating fresh, cold, white grapes. Quench your thirst on a hot day.

The Reds

Pinot Noir - The great grape of Burgundy, France shows up in a light to medium-bodied style in Michigan with hints of black berries, cassis, earth and spice. Enjoy with grilled lamb, moussaka, braised venison, grilled salmon.

Marechal Foch - A French-American hybrid grape that bottles as a light to medium-bodied wine with a delightful nose and palate of candied cherries and raspberries. Terrific with pizza or pasta.

Chancellor - Medium-bodied red with a nose of berries, and some soft tannins give this red more depth than Foch. Enjoy with meat-based pasta sauces and Italian cuisine (lasagna Bolognese, manicotti), roast duck, roast turkey, grilled tuna steaks.

Michigan Cherry Wine - Dry style is wonderful with roast duck; sweet style can be dessert, or enjoyed alongside Black Forest cake, flourless chocolate cake, or cheesecake. Reduce the sweet wine in a saucepan and drizzle over grilled venison chops, roast duck, pork dishes, or ice cream. 🍷

Recipes

By Jill A. Ditmire

Country Shells with Venison Sausage
(Serves 4-6)

1 T	olive oil
1	carrot, peeled and diced
1	celery stalk, diced
1	sweet onion, diced
1 pound	ground venison or venison sausage removed from casings (can substitute sweet Italian sausage)
1/2 cup	Chancellor
1	16 oz can plum tomatoes with juice
2 T	tomato paste
1 pound	pasta shells (rigatoni or ziti)
1 cup	cooked white cannelloni beans, rinsed
1 bunch	leaf spinach, stems removed, washed and roughly chopped (or 10 oz. thawed, drained, frozen chopped spinach)
1/4 cup	grated Parmesan cheese

salt and pepper

Place a large skillet over medium high heat and add the oil. When hot, add carrot, celery and onion. Cook till vegetables soften, about 7 minutes. Add ground venison and cook till no longer pink, but not browned. Reduce heat to medium low and add wine, tomatoes and juice, and tomato paste. Simmer until sauce thickens, about 20 minutes. Add beans, spinach, salt, pepper.

Prepare pasta according to directions on box.

Toss the cooked pasta with the sauce, adding cheese and stirring till spinach wilts and mixture is heated through. Serve immediately.

WINE: Enjoy with a glass of Chancellor or Marechal Foch. Both red wines pair nicely with the earthy rich flavors of the venison, spinach and beans.

Chilled Michigan Cherry Soup
(Makes 10 first course or dessert servings)

15 pounds Michigan Bing Cherries, pitted and
de-stemmed
1 bottle Michigan Pinot Noir (can also substitute
Michigan Marechal Foch)
1 Cinnamon stick
1/4 cup corn starch
1/4 cup water
1/2 cup Michigan Cherry Honey

In a large soup pot over medium heat, combine cherries, wine and cinnamon. Bring to a boil and simmer for 15 minutes. Purée in small batches in food processor or use hand held burr mixer. Strain purée through a colander and return to pot. Bring to a boil. In small bowl combine corn starch and water and blend to make a slurry. Slowly pour slurry into boiling purée, stirring constantly until mixture thickens slightly (enough to coat the back of a spoon). Remove from heat. Stir in honey, adding more if soup is still a bit tart. Chill.

Serve in individual bowls with a dollop of sour cream as a first course, or with dollops of crème fraîche as a dessert.

WINE: This tangy, tart soup is excellent as a first course with a glass of the Michigan wine (Pinot Noir, Marechal Foch) used in the recipe. When serving as a dessert, accompany with a glass of Late Harvest Riesling or Sweet Cherry Wine.

Green Apple Risotto with Cabbage and Bacon
(Serves 4 as a side dish)

1/2 cup	chopped high quality thick-sliced bacon
2	garlic cloves, chopped
1/2 head	Savoy cabbage, thinly sliced
1 tsp	kosher salt
1 tsp	ground black pepper
1 1/2 cups	Arborio rice
3 1/2 cups	water
1 1/2 cups	apple cider
1	Granny Smith apple, peeled, cored and chopped into dice
1 T Dijon	mustard
1/3 cup	chopped scallions
2 T	unsalted butter at room temperature

Heat a heavy-bottomed large saucepan over medium heat. When hot, add bacon and cook till bacon renders fat. Add garlic, cabbage, salt, pepper stirring well after each addition. Cook till cabbage wilts, about 10 minutes. Add rice and stir till well coated.

Stirring constantly, add 1 cup water and cook until water is absorbed by rice. Continue stirring and add half of the cider. When absorbed, continue adding water and cider 1 cup at a time, until all water and cider is added and absorbed–about 18 to 20 minutes. Stir constantly during this process.

Add apple, mustard, scallions and butter. Stir and serve immediately.

WINE: This dish yearns to be paired with either a Michigan dry style Riesling or Pinot Gris. The flavors in both wines echo the flavors of the dish. Both on the plate and in the glass you will experience luscious layers of rich buttery flavor balanced by crisp, tart fruit. A match made in heaven!

How Wine Is Made

This section is intended to be a very brief overview.

Winemaking

The winemaker is the person who turns grapes into wine. **Enology** is the science of wines and winemaking. An enologist has earned a degree in the science of winemaking. **Viticulture** is the science, or art, of grape growing. **Vinification** is the process of turning grape juice into wine.

Grape Harvest

Harvest time can vary, occassionally beginning in late August and, in Michigan, sometimes extending into November. Harvest is a winery's busiest season, and those wineries that cultivate their own grapes usually work around the clock. Grapes can be picked by machine or by hand, and are then transported to the winery as quickly as possible. **Sulphur dioxide** will be added when the grapes are crushed to prevent spoilage and to kill wild yeasts.

Red Wine

The red grapes are not harvested until they are as ripe as possible. The fruit's ripeness is an important factor in the quality of the red wine. It is the skin of the red-wine grapes that gives the wine its color, tannin and the many fruit flavors that red wine lovers enjoy. Once the grapes have been picked, the under-ripe and rotten ones are discarded. The grapes are then lightly crushed into a thick mush, called '**must**,' and all stalks are removed. The must is then transferred into stainless steel tanks or oak barrels. The grapes may sit in their juices and soften for hours or even days before the winemaker begins the **fermentation**. This process is called '**cold soaking**'.

Fermentation occurs when yeast cells convert the sugar in the juice into alcohol. Using cultured yeast, the winemaker sets the temperature in the tanks at 77-86 degrees Fahrenheit. Converting all of the sugar into alcohol usually takes less than two weeks.

Most red wines and some white wines go through a second 'malolactic' fermentation in which the sharper malic acid is converted to lactic acid. The new wine may be left to sit on the skins for one to four weeks after the first fermentation. During this time, the color will redden and the tannin will soften. (**Tannin** is in the skin of the red grape and gives an astringent taste to the wine. This astringency is magnified if the wine is chilled when it is consumed–so most red wines are served at room temperature.)

Finally, the wine is drawn from the tank. The first wine is called the **free-run**, because it freely runs out of the tank.

The remaining wine, which contains slightly more tannin, is squeezed out by a winepress. It is then mixed in with the free-run juice (in proportions chosen by the individual winemaker) in order to adjust the tannin level in the wine. The wine is clarified to rid it of solids and remove any cloudiness. Finally, the wine is placed in stainless steel tanks or oak barrels to age. When it reaches the determined maturation date, the wine is bottled.

How long should wine age? Some wine is sold immediately to the consumer. If the winery is producing a fine wine, it could sit for one year or more before distribution.

It is a misconception that wine, red or white, aged in oak is better than wine aged in stainless steel. This is a matter of individual taste. (Tastes associated with oak aging are nutmeg, vanilla, chocolate or smoke.)

White Wine

It is trickier for the winemaker to make a good white wine than to make a good red wine. The white grape skins are thin and, consequently, can rot faster or overcook in the sun. Because the fruit must be harvested at just the right time, it becomes a delicate balancing act between too soon and too late.

White grapes go to the pressing machines, and the grape juice is immediately separated from the skins and stems. (For Chardonnay and Gewürztraminer, the juice may be left in contact with the skins for a longer time.) The juice is now ready for fermentation, which takes place at a cooler temperature–50-70 degrees Fahrenheit.

The lower temperatures create a light, crisp wine. Yet, the warmer the temperature, the fuller the wine. The rest of the process is essentially the same as for red wines.

Rosé–or a more modern name–Blush Wine

Blush wines are made from red grapes, but with the same processing as white wines. The juice is allowed a very short period of contact, usually a few hours, with the skins before they're removed–giving blush its 'pink' color.

From Dry to Sweet

When all the sugar in the grapes has been converted to alcohol, the wine is said to be dry. However, there are ways of keeping some residual sugar. The winemaker can filter out the yeast whenever desired during the process. Sterilized unfermented juice may be added back at the end. The result is that any grape can be made to produce a wine as sweet or dry as desired.

Blending the Grapes

Many wines–both red and white–are blends of different grape varieties. Different wines can be fermented separately and then brought together later. The winemaker can blend different barrels of wine from the same grape variety, or wines from different vineyards, or even different regions, to create one kind of wine before bottling. Blending is an age-old tradition just about anywhere that you can find a winemaker.

Sparkling Wines

Traditional sparkling wines are made from a combination of red- and white-skinned grapes. The winemaking production method begins the same as with still wine–the grapes are pressed quickly and then fermented to create a dry wine. Red grapes are treated as they are for blush wines.

When grape juice ferments, carbon dioxide gas is released into the atmosphere. However, if the winemaker wants to produce sparkling wine, the carbon dioxide gas must be prevented from escaping. So the winemaker takes the wine, adds a controlled amount of sugar and yeast, and induces a second fermentation in a closed container.

The two methods that are used to make sparkling wines are the **Methode Champenoise**, a traditional method of second fermentation in the bottle, and the **Charmat** method, in which carbon dioxide gas is trapped in the tank and fermentation takes place there.

If the winemaker is using the Champenoise method to make the sparkling wine, the wine stays in the same bottle from the second fermentation until it is sold. The bottles are left untouched for months–or even years–for the higher quality sparkling wines. During this time, a slow a process called autolysis takes place. The spent yeast cells come in contact with the wine in the bottle and are slowly destroyed by their own enzymes. The **autolysis** process is important to the taste factor. The longer the yeast is in contact with the wine, the more the flavor takes on the yeast characteristics.

There is another important factor in the length of time the sparkling wine is aged. In the second fermentation, the carbon dioxide is trapped. The longer the wine sits, the more the gas becomes incorporated into the wine, and the more slowly it is released from the wine in the glass.

There are still sediments left in the wine, so winemakers use a method called **riddling**, a gentle turning of the bottles by hand, to get the sediments to settle onto the cap and eventually pop out. The neck of the bottle is submerged in a solution with temperatures below freezing. The idea is to freeze the sediment resting upon the cap into an ice plug. Once frozen, the winemaker turns the bottle up and pops off the cap. The sediment, trapped in its ice cube, shoots out of the bottle. The bottle is then resealed with the champagne cork.

The entire Champenoise method is very time consuming and labor intensive and is reserved for the higher quality grape varieties. 🍷

GLOSSARY OF WINE TERMS

Acidic A wine that is unbalanced; tending to have too much acid, making it sharp, sour or tart.

Aftertaste (or Finish) The lingering impression of the taste of the wine after swallowing. It may be short, lingering, long, clean, dirty, or have other pleasant or unpleasant features.

Appellation See Viticultural Area.

Aroma The scents or odors associated with the initial making of the wine. The grape variety, fermentation practices and aging in newer oak are the chief elements of aroma. These are present in young wines and tend to disappear with aging.

Balance Refers to the proportion or harmony of the various elements of wine taste such as fruit, oak, acid, sweetness and tannin.

Barnyard The smell and flavor of wines infected with the brettanomyces strain of yeast, and appreciated by some.

Barrel-fermented Refers to the fermentation of a wine in small oak barrels rather than in a tank. See Sur-Lie

Bell Pepper An aroma associated with less-than-fully ripe members of the Cabernet family of grapes.

Bland A wine that has little character or taste; generally low in acid and tannin; insipid.

Body The tactile impression of fullness on the palate due to alcohol, glycerin and residual sugar as well as extract.

Bouquet The scents or odors that originate from aging. Bouquet emerges as the wine matures.

Breathing Allowing a wine to stand open–preferably in a decanter–for an hour or two before being consumed. This may have the effect of dissipating off odors and mellowing or enhancing flavors.

Complex(ity) A wine containing many different aromas, bouquets and flavors, producing a pleasing harmony.

Corky (Corked) A wine that has a musty or dank smell caused by an infected cork. It is not actually harmful. People vary in their ability to detect this and other wine faults.

Dry A wine that contains little or no residual sugar; the absence of sweetness.

Earthy A wine that smells like freshly turned soil, an aroma that usually adds to the pleasant complexity of the wine.

Extract The non-sugar wine solids dissolved in alcohol which contribute to its weight and body.

Fermentation The process of converting sugars to ethyl alcohol by yeasts in the juice of fruits or vegetables. Carbon dioxide is also a by-product of this process. See Malolactic Fermentation.

Filtered A wine clarified by use of a filter to remove yeasts, bacteria and other particulate matter that can detract from appearance and quality.

Fining A clarifying technique that introduces an electrolytic agent such as egg whites, gelatin, bentonite clay or one of many other agents to instantly bond with unwanted solids in the wine. These will settle to the bottom of the tank before removing the clean wine (racking) and do not remain a part of the finished wine.

Finish See Aftertaste.

Fortified A wine to which brandy has been added to increase alcoholic strength to 18-21%. This is often used to retain residual sugar as well.

Foxy The strong "grapey" aroma of native American (vitis labrusca) grape varieties; the smell of Concord, Niagara and similar grapes and the wines, juices and jellies made from them. There is no agreed upon explanation of the origin of this term.

French-American Hybrids Hybrids or crosses between native American grape varieties and varieties of European vitis vinifera. These are usually more cold- and disease-resistant than vinifera and have a more traditional taste than native varieties. Seyval Blanc and Vidal Blanc are typical examples. Not all hybrids have names, but all have numbers–e.g. Seyval Blanc is SV5276.

Fruity The fragrance or flavor of young wines that are especially aromatic; but also the fragrance of wines that smell decisively of the grape variety from which they were made. Sometimes confused with sweetness; but fruity wines can also be dry.

Full-bodied The feel in the mouth when a wine is high in alcohol and/or extract.

Generic A wine made to imitate famous wine regions, such as Chablis or Burgundy, and by extension, any cheap or nondescript wine.

Grafting The process of getting one variety of plant to grow on the root or trunk of another variety. Nearly all varieties of grapes today are planted on a limited number of hybrid rootstocks. See Rootstock.

Grassy Green, floral aromas, e.g., freshly mown hay, cut grass, etc.

Herbaceous Smelling like or reminiscent of herbs.

Hybrid See French-American hybrid.

Ice Wine A wine made from grapes which have been frozen. The remaining concentrated juice makes an intense and sweet dessert wine.

Labrusca See vitis labrusca.

Lake Effect The process by which westerly winds off the Great Lakes lengthen the growing season and bring winter snow cover to vineyards within 30 miles of their shores.

Lees The sediment that accumulates after fermentation in a tank or barrel. It usually consists of dead yeast cells and proteins.

Legs The "tears," or streams, of wine that cling to the sides of the glass after swirling. This is caused by differential evaporation of alcohol and other liquids in the wine. It generally indicates higher alcoholic content and body.

Maderized A color and flavor change due to the storing of a wine at too high a temperature. Consists of brownish coloration and loss of fruit flavors with development of varying degrees of caramel, or even shoe polish, odors. Named after the island of Madeira whose famous fortified wines mature at high temperatures.

Malolactic Fermentation A secondary fermentation caused by bacteria that convert malic acid (a sharp acid) to lactic acid (a softer acid). This is done to soften a wine's acidity. This does not occur in all wines.

Methode Champenoise The traditional method of producing sparkling wine by causing a secondary fermentation in the bottle instead of in a tank. This produces the highest quality sparkling wines.

Microclimate Often used to refer to the vineyard site and surrounding area. The correct term is mesoclimate. True microclimate is the zone within and immediately surrounding an individual vine.

Native Varieties Refers to grape varieties of the various species of grapes native to North America–especially vitis labrusca.

Nutty Aromas or bouquets reminiscent of nuts.

Oak Aging The maturing of wines usually in smaller oak barrels, as opposed to stainless steel or glass. These barrels may be old or new, made from various types of oak, be toasted inside to various degrees, be kiln or air dried and differ in other ways as well, all of which influence the taste of the wine stored in them.

Off-Dry A wine that is only slightly sweet or almost dry.

Oxidized The smell, taste and color of an oxygen-exposed wine. The color will become orange or brown, and the smell and flavor less fresh and more like sherry, caramel, nuts or shoe polish.

Phylloxera A vine-killing root louse that has infected the world's vineyards necessitating that nearly all vines be grafted to resistant hybrid rootstocks. Native American varieties and many of their hybrids are immune.

Proprietary A wine name that is privately owned as opposed to one that names a grape variety or viticultural area.

Residual Sugar The unfermented sugars in a wine at bottling, either expressed as grams/liter or as a percentage.

Racking The process of drawing off or siphoning off clean wine to separate it from sediment or the lees in a barrel or tank.

Rich The full flavors of a wine.

Robust The character of a full-bodied, full-flavored wine that is heavy and tannic.

Rootstock Nearly all modern grapevines are grown on the roots of a limited number of hybrid varieties that have been developed to resist the phylloxera root louse. Only hybrid vines are capable of surviving on their own roots. See Phylloxera.

Round A wine that is smooth and gentle due to a particular alcohol/acid/tannin balance that smoothes the sharpness of the acids and tannins, making the wine feel "round" in the mouth.

Sediment Deposits precipitated in the bottle by an aged wine.

Semi-dry Similar to off-dry.

Semi-sweet A wine that is slightly, or somewhat sweet.

Sparkling Wines The correct name for wines that contain carbon dioxide bubbles. Normally this occurs by a secondary fermentation in a closed container. Not all of these wines are Champagne, because this is the name of a region in France. See Methode Champenoise

Spicy A wine with aromas and flavors that evoke an impression of spice.

Sur-Lie Refers to leaving the newly fermented wine with the lees of fermentation in order to create more body and complexity.

Sweet This term may either indicate that the wine contains perceptible sugar or, more often, that it is sweeter than semi sweet.

Table Wine Legally, any wine containing less than 14% alcohol. Otherwise used to signify a drier wine to be served with food; in contrast to fortified or dessert wines.

Tannic A wine relatively high in tannin, making it bitter or astringent; often young, barrel-aged red wines.

Tannin A bitter, astringent acid derived from skins, seeds and wooden barrels that causes a puckery sensation in the mouth and throat. Since the color of red wines comes from the skins of red-skinned grapes, this is a common feature of many intense red wines. Tannin dissipates with time, thus the recommendation that red wines need to age.

Unbalanced A wine lacking harmony among its acid, sugar, fruit, oak or tannin components, usually with one dominating the others.

Varietal Refers to a wine named after the grape variety from which it was principally made; and to wines that exemplify to a high degree the typical attributes of a variety.

Vegetal Any odor of vegetables or leafy substances, e.g., asparagus or green bean.

Vinegary The smell or taste of acetic acid, which is the result of bacterial contamination. Harmless and even attractive in very small amounts, an excess is a serious and uncommon fault.

Viticultural Area (Appellation/Denomination) A delimited region where common geographical or climatic attributes contribute to a unique and definable character in the wine. American Viticultural Areas (AVAs) are approved by the federal government. In Europe, appellations and denominations may also mandate grape varieties, ripeness levels, crop levels and more.

vitis labrusca A species of grapes native to North America that are winter-hardy and disease-resistant. Close relatives Concord and Niagara are familiar examples now used principally for juices and jams.

vitis vinifera The only species of grapes native to Europe. The thousands of varieties of vitis vinifera are used to make the finest wines in the world. Chardonnay, Pinot Noir and Riesling are well-known examples.

Vinifera See vitis vinifera.

Wine The product of the fermentation of grapes or other fruits or vegetables.

Michigan Grape Varieties

Baco Noir A red French-American hybrid grape capable of producing complex and elegant wines.

Cabernet Franc A red vinifera grape similar to Cabernet Sauvignon, but which ripens earlier, is more perfumed and less astringent.

Cabernet Sauvignon A high-quality, late-ripening red vinifera grape producing medium- to full-bodied wines often with considerable astringency.

Catawba A deep pink-skinned, fruity, native American grape, once the backbone of the American wine industry.

Cayuga A white French-American hybrid grape that can make attractive light-bodied, aromatic wines.

Chambourcin A red French-American hybrid grape that produces medium- to full-bodied wines of considerable character.

Chancellor A red French-American hybrid grape that produces rich, soft aromatic wines.

Chardonel A white French-American hybrid of Chardonnay and Seyval Blanc. It produces high-quality wines similar to, but slightly lighter than, Chardonnay.

Chardonnay A white vinifera grape that produces medium- to full-bodied wines that can attain very high quality. Aging in newer oak barrels is common.

Concord A full-bodied, aromatic, red native American grape used mostly for juice.

De Chaunac A red French-American hybrid grape, named after a pioneering viticulturist, that produces sound, lighter-bodied wines.

Gamay A red vinifera grape producing attractive, medium-bodied wines.

Gewürztraminer A very aromatic, pink vinifera grape that produces very high quality, spicy wines in both dry and sweeter styles.

Leon Millot A very early-ripening, red French-American hybrid grape that produces big flavorful wines.

Marechal Foch A very early-ripening, red French-American hybrid grape, named after the French general, that is capable of producing very attractive medium-bodied wines.

Vinifera Varieties

Pinot Gris

Pinot Noir

Chardonnay

Merlot A red vinifera grape that can produce full-bodied, soft wines.

Niagara An aromatic, white native American grape used mostly for juice.

Pinot Blanc A white vinifera grape that produces very attractive, lighter-bodied wines.

Pinot Grigio/Gris A versatile pink vinifera grape that produces wines ranging from very light to very rich and flavorful. Grigio is the Italian name; Gris, the French. The name means "grey" though we would call the grape's color pink.

Pinot Meunier A red vinifera grape, used mostly for sparkling wine, that gets its name from the whitish cast of its leaves. A "meunier" is someone who grinds flour.

Pinot Noir A red vinifera grape capable of producing some of the finest medium- to full-bodied red and sparkling wines in the world.

Riesling An aromatic and extremely versatile white vinifera grape capable of producing some of the world's finest ageworthy white wines in styles ranging from dry to very sweet, and sparkling as well. Also called Johannisberg/Johannesburg Riesling and White Riesling.

Seyval Blanc A white French-American hybrid grape producing light, crisp wines.

Traminette A white French-American hybrid grape producing light- to medium-bodied, spicy wines.

Vidal Blanc An aromatic, white French-American hybrid grape that produces attractive, fruity wines.

Vignoles A white French-American hybrid grape that often retains considerable acidity and is capable of producing superb semi-dry and dessert wines.

Resistant Varieties

Chancellor

Vignoles

Marechal
Foch

How To Read A Wine Label

Ciccone Vineyard & Winery
the name of the winery

Gewürztraminer
the name of the grape variety from which the wine was made. By law, a maximum of 25% may be from some other variety.

Estate bottled
all the grapes were grown, and the wine made and bottled by the winery.

Table wine
indicates that the wine contains between 7% and 14% alcohol. The winery could list the exact amount instead.

Leelanau Peninsula
the wine's appellation; the federally approved 'American Viticultural Area' where the grapes were grown.

1999
the 'vintage' or year in which the grapes were harvested.

TRILLIUM

A proprietary blend of white wines
from Michigan's Leelanau Peninsula.
Semi Dry White Table Wine

Produced and Bottled By Good Harbor Vineyards, Lake Leelanau, MI 49653

Trillium
the name of the wine. This
name is the property of the
winery and no one else can
use it, so the name is 'proprietary.'

Leelanau Peninsula
the wine's appellation

Semi-dry
indicates there is some
residual sugar in the
wine

Table wine
the wine contains
between 7% and 14%
alcohol

Produced and bottled
indicates that the winery may have
purchased some of the grapes for this
wine, however, the winery vinified
the wine and bottled it.

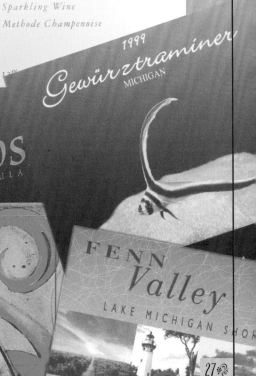

The Art of Wine Tasting

Visual

To really examine a wine, hold a glassful in the air against either light from a window, a white background, or a lamp. The color of the wine changes depending on the particular grape variety. Wines with deep color are usually fuller tasting. In a red wine, the purple color indicates a young wine and a red-brown indicates an older vintage. As for white wines, a young wine will be nearly colorless and an aged white wine will be a gold or deep gold color.

Smelling or Sniffing

Pour about one to two ounces of wine in your glass, hold it by the stem and swirl the wine to release the aromas. After you swirl, put your nose to the rim and deep into the glass, making the upper rim touch the bridge of your nose. You will smell fruity, spicy, or wood odors.

Swirl

Gently swirl the wine in the glass to release the aromas and let it air out before tasting it.

Tasting

When you are wine tasting, it is better to taste the white wines before the red wines, dry before sweet wines, and older vintages before young wines. Swish a mouthful of wine around so it touches all sides of your tongue and the roof of your mouth. If you are sampling a dry red wine, aerate it by imitating the motion of whistling backward to draw in air with the wine in your mouth. The air should change the taste in your mouth.

Spitting

If you are touring many wineries, it is advisable to spit–and don't be shy about it. Wineries do not take offense at this and often have a bucket for you to spit in. If you are shy about spitting, just take a sip and leave the rest. Then ask for just a taste of additional samples.

Storing

When storing wine, the cork must be kept moist. The bottle should be placed on its side or upside down. Wine should be kept in a room that is cool, 55-65 degrees Fahrenheit, and should not be exposed to heat or direct sunlight.

Serving

Before serving champagne or sparkling wine, it is good to chill it for three hours at 40 degrees Fahrenheit. White wines should chill for two hours at 45-50 degrees Fahrenheit. Red wine is served at room temperature, usually 60-65 degrees Fahrenheit, and should be opened to air for one hour before serving. Air softens the tannins and intensifies the bouquet.

SOUTHWEST WINERIES

N

Muskegon

Gran

196

40

89

37

131

40

89

31

Benton Harbor

40

St. Joseph

94

Lemon Creek
Winery

51

40

Heart
of the
Vineyard
Winery

Tabor Hill
Winery

94

31

12

TOUR 1
Southwest Region

*Lakeshore and Fennville are two
of the four federally approved American
Viticultural Areas in Michigan. The latitude and
climate along Michigan's lakeshore are similar to
Oregon and Washington State. It's breezy and
warm, allowing wineries along this shoreline
to grow wine grapes such as Pinot Grigio (also
known as Pinot Gris), Riesling, Pinot Noir and
Merlot. In the Southwestern region you can visit
eight wineries that we have connected as a tour.
Enjoy the drive along the shoreline and the
beautiful sunsets to complete a romantic trip.
Most of all, have fun and enjoy the wine.*

Tour 1 — Heart of the Vineyard

Tabor Hill Winery

Tabor Hill Winery is located in Buchanan. From the Chicago area take I-94 east to Exit 16 north toward Bridgman. Turn right on Red Arrow Highway, then right on Lake St. (Lake becomes Shawnee Road.) Follow Shawnee to Hills Road, turn right and follow the signs to the winery.

Tabor Hill Winery sits on a hilltop surrounded by their luscious, sprawling 50 acres of vineyards. The setting couldn't be more picturesque. The tasting room is like a country house with a patio for summer tourists to lounge and sip their delicious Grand Mark Sparkling Wine while taking in the rich and colorful vineyards. This winery has got to be on everyone's Michigan tour list.

In 1981 Dave and Linda Upton purchased Tabor Hill Winery and brought it to its current state of success. In the late 1960s five men from the Gary steel mills became suddenly unemployed and sought backers to grow wine grapes–both the Concord and viniferas such as Riesling and Chardonnay. They were thought to be reckless for trying to grow viniferas in Michigan by other wine grape growers in the Midwest. However, they did succeed, through trial and error.

Tabor Hill grows 11 different kinds of wine grapes (mostly viniferas) in their vineyards. Presently they grow Chardonnay, Pinot Noir, Merlot, Seyval, Vignoles and Chardonnel. The majority of their wine is produced from their vineyards.

Mike Merchant, a veteran winemaker for over

18 years, and his wines, are testament to many years of study and hard work. The first on your must-try list is their fine, crisp Grand Mark Sparkling Wine made of Pinot Noir and Chardonnay. This sparkling wine won a gold medal at the 2000 Michigan State Fair wine judging. A personal favorite is their 1999 Lake Michigan Shore Cabernet Franc, with a soft raspberry aroma and a slightly peppery finish. For a white wine, try the Lake Michigan Shore Chardonnay, which has a buttery, nutty flavor with a hint of oak. This wine moves over the palate smoothly. Don't forget to try the dry Riesling.

Take in the majestic scenery at Tabor Hill by arriving around lunch or dinnertime and enjoy a meal in their acclaimed restaurant. This is by far one of the best restaurants in the area. The Duck Breast marinated in Riesling and topped with tart blueberry Bigarade sauce and the Raspberry Chicken are the house specialties.

They also have tasting rooms in Bridgman and Saugatuck.

Tabor Hill Winery

185 Mount Tabor Road
Buchanan, MI 49107
Tel: (800) 283-3363
Fax: (616) 422-2787

www.taborhill.com

Hours:

Mon & Tues: 10am to 5pm
Wed–Sat: 10am to 10pm
Sun: Noon to 9pm

Winter Hours:
Mon–Thurs: 10am to 5pm
Fri. & Sat: Noon to 9pm
Sun: Noon to 5pm

Heart of the Vineyard

Go back to Hills Road and turn right. Follow Hills Road until you see the winery sign. You can't miss the round barn, the winery's trademark.

This is an unusual Amish round barn built in 1911. It is used to house the winery's distillery for fruit brandies as well as for special events. In fact, this barn is the site for many weddings. The wine tasting room is in an 1881 post-and-beam barn. These two architectural wonders sit in a rustic atmosphere surrounded by bountiful vineyards–just minutes away from the Warren Dunes.

Entering the winery is like taking a walk into the past. Rick and Sherrie Moersch own Heart of the Vineyard. Rick is the main winemaker and began his winemaking career with Tabor Hill Winery, first as a consultant, then general manager. He was previously a biology teacher, and the chemical process of making wine came quite naturally to him. In 1992, the Moersches opened their own winery.

There are 12 acres of fruit grown on their well-drained, fertile soil which gives way to some of the best white wine in this part of the country. From their tasting room, try the Chardonnay Reserve, with a perfect balance of buttery fruit flavor and only hints of oak. A must-try is the Vineyard Tears, a Vin d'Alsace, with floral aromas, and made with riper and more scented fruit. Red wine lovers will enjoy sampling their Merlot, which has been aged three years in French-American oak and has a full berry fruit flavor. Don't miss the Artesia Sauvage, a dry, French-style sparkling wine, aged three years.

Heart of the Vineyard Winery

10983 Hills Road
Baroda, MI 49101
Tel: (800) 716-9463
Fax: (616) 422-5038

www.heartofthevineyard.com

Hours:
Mon.–Sat: 10am to 6pm
Sun: Noon to 6pm
Open year-round

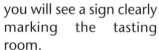

Lemon Creek Vineyards and Winery

From Heart of the Vineyard, take a right out of the driveway onto Hills Road. Take a left at the stop sign at the corner and go straight through the next stop sign. Turn right at Singer Lake Road, and another right onto Lemon Creek Road. Lemon Creek Winery is about half a mile on the left.

When you first approach the grounds, you feel as though you are in a neighborhood, with the winery sandwiched in between two quaint houses. Drive just past the houses and

you will see a sign clearly marking the tasting room.

This fifth generation of farmers grows over 100 acres of wine grapes, making it by far the largest Southwest Michigan vineyard. The Lemons homesteaded on this land in 1855. They spent many years growing grapes, both viniferas and French hybrids, for other wineries in the Midwest. It wasn't until 1984 that they made their own mark with their estate-grown wines.

While you are there, the requisite on the list of many estate wines to try is the '98 Chardonnay–a dry white, aged in American oak for 18 months. Their Barrel Select Red is a blend of Chambourcin, Chancellor and Cabernet. The Cabernet Sauvignon is a gold medal winner. The Lemons' tasting room also offers semi-sweet wines, such as Lighthouse White–a rich, fruity wine. Have it with dessert, and you won't be sorry.

They offer sparkling juices with no alcohol or added sugar if you want to take the kids along.

Lemon Creek Vineyards and Winery

533 E. Lemon Creek Road
Berrien Springs, MI 49103
Tel: (616) 471-1321
Fax: (616) 471-1322

Hours:
May–October and December
Mon.–Sat: 9am to 6pm
Sun: Noon to 6pm

November–April
Fri.–Sun: Noon to 5pm

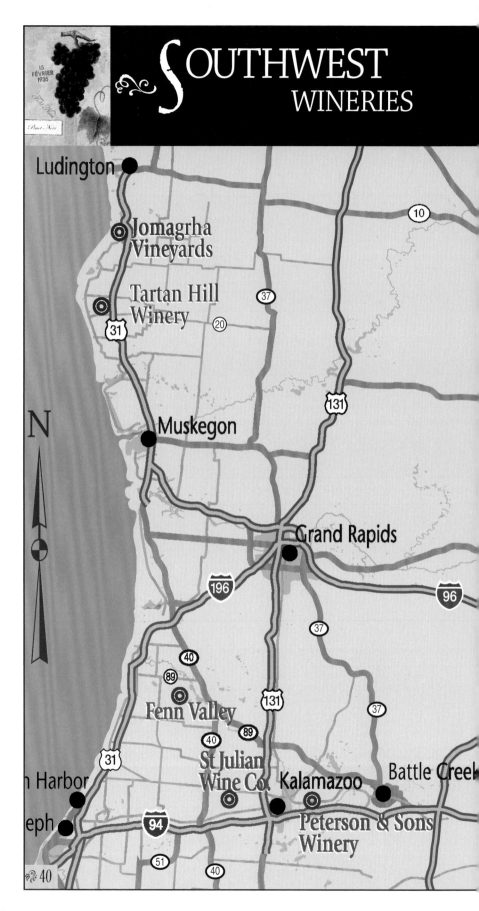

Ludington

Jomagrha Vineyards

Tartan Hill Winery

N

Muskegon

Grand Rapids

Fenn Valley

St Julian Wine Co

Kalamazoo

Battle Creek

n Harbor

eph

Peterson & Sons Winery

TOUR 2
Southwest Region

St. Julian Wine Company vintage grape presses

St. Julian Wine Company

S t. Julian is located in Paw Paw, Michigan. Take I-94 east toward Paw Paw/Kalamazoo to exit 60 (Lawton/Paw Paw north). Go about 1/2 mile and it is on the left on the main street.

St. Julian Winery was named after the patron saint of the village of Falaria in Italy, where the founder was born. Michigan's oldest winery set its stake in the ground in 1934, following the era of prohibition.

David Braganini, the third generation of the winery's leadership, now operates the 80-year-old business. All wine is produced from Michigan-grown grapes. Because of their large volume of wine production, St. Julian contracts with other vineyards to procure the best grapes in Michigan. "They pick their contractors as carefully as they make their wine," says Chas Catherman, the winery's chief winemaker.

The tasting room is spacious and welcoming with a wine tasting counter to accommodate 20 or more. The wine servers are helpful and knowledgeable about all of the wine they are serving. The winery houses a hip reception room that was once a full-time restaurant. They hold many weddings and events here.

Take a tour through the amazingly modern facility. They not only bottle and label their own wine, but they bottle other wineries' wines as well, employing the latest technologies.

Their biggest seller is the Solera Cream Sherry, aged in a true Solera System and a winner of many gold medals. A new wine on the must-try list is the La Niña 1999, a Bordeaux-style blend of Cabernet Sauvignon, Cabernet Franc and Merlot. La Niña is robust and full of chocolate and raspberry. White wine lovers, don't miss the Michigan Chardonnay 1998, a wine that has been matured in small barrels and is full of peach and lemon aromas. For dessert wines, their pear or raspberry fruit infusions are a blend of fruit juices with brandy made of the same fruit.

St. Julian Winery began a big expansion with tasting rooms added around southern Michigan–in Frankenmuth, Dundee, Parma, and Union Pier. The tasting rooms are well-advertised, so watch for the signs in these areas. All are open year-round.

St. Julian Wine Company

716 S. Kalamazoo St.
Paw Paw, MI 49079
Tel: (800) 732-6002
Fax: (616) 657-5743

www.stjulian.com

Hours:
Open year-round
Mon–Sat: 9am to 5pm
Sun: Noon to 5pm
(Tasting room hours vary)

Peterson and Sons Winery

Take I-94 east to exit 85 (35th Street). Turn right and go south on 35th St. for approximately five miles and look for signs.

Peterson and Sons sings a different tune from most wineries. It is one of the few wineries in the world to make wine without added chemicals or preservatives. If you're allergic to sulfites or other additives, you'll want to give these a try. Duane Peterson, the proprietor, made the world's first-known grape washing machine to clean the grapes before crushing, to rid them of sprays, insects, and bad grapes and their vinegar spores.

The Petersons buy all of their grapes from Michigan farmers. These wines do taste different because of the lack of chemicals. They ferment the whole fruit for an extended period of time–up to two weeks–and they don't filter the juice. They win medals each year for their wines.

While you are there, try the Chambourcin, a dry red wine, or the Niagara, an off-dry white. Petersons' fruit wine list is extensive, and includes unusual varieties like Black Raspberry and Rhubarb-Cherry. Regular customers keep the winery very busy. Peterson says he sells out every year.

Peterson and Sons Winery

9375 East P Avenue
Kalamazoo, MI 49001
Tel: (616) 626-9755

www.kalamazoomi.com

Hours:

Open year-round
Mon, Fri, and Sat: 10am to 6pm
Sun: Noon to 6pm

Fenn Valley Vineyards

Fenn Valley Vineyards

Go back to I-94 toward Kalamazoo and go north on US-31 to the M-89 Otsego/Plainwell exit. Take M-89 through Allegan toward Fennville. Pass through Fennville and drive 1.5 miles to 62nd Street, turn left and go to the first crossroad, 122nd Ave., and again turn left. The winery is 1/4 mile down the road on the right.

Like most Michigan wineries, Fenn Valley is family-owned and operated. Founded in 1973 by a brother and sister team, Doug and Diana Welsch, it's one of the old-

est in Michigan. The family's 55 acres of vineyards are surrounded by land producing abundant fruit orchards. The Welsches migrated from Chicago and chose their land judiciously. The vineyards are located on the top of a large sand ridge between the Black River and Kalamazoo River valleys, and inland from Lake Michigan. This is an ideal spot for wine grapes due to the lake's moderation of winter temperatures—and during the summer months the lake gives off a cool breeze that the viniferas thrive on. Because the vineyards are on the rolling hills, the land is well-drained during both the summer and winter months.

The winery is a newly built hacienda-like structure with large Spanish-style wooden doors. Upon entering, you will be welcomed by a spacious wine bar surrounded by racks and racks of wine. Once outside, take a few minutes to view the scenery of verdant hills bursting with orchards and vineyards. The Welsches are making this winery very com-

fortable for tourists to come and enjoy their wine and surroundings without feeling intimidated.

Fenn Valley Vineyards yield viniferas such as Riesling, Chardonnay and Pinot Noir, and premium hybrids such as Seyval, Chancellor and Chambourcin. The winery's most popular wine is the Capriccio, a soft red wine with a nice balance between fruitiness and acidity. This won a Best in Show at the Michigan State Fair in 1999. For an excellent white wine, try the 2000 Dry Riesling, a premium white with floral undertones and a touch of oak. You can taste the lemon and green apple fruit characteristics.

One of the winery's specialties is the Vineyard Nectar 1996–a wine made of concentrated grape juice that comes very close to being an ice wine. Vineyard Nectar is very popular with tourists as well as with the locals.

Watch for special events that are held each year, especially the wine tasting out in the fields. You will find yourself immersed in the grapes. What a great idea and a lot of fun!

Fenn Valley Vineyards

6130 122nd Ave.
Fennville, MI 49408
Tel: (616) 561-2396 or
Phone: (800) 432-6265
Fax: (616) 561-2973

www.fennvalley.com

Hours:

Open year-round
Mon.–Sat: 10am to 5pm
Sun: 1pm to 5pm
June, Sept. and Oct.,
Fri. and Sat: 10am to 5:30pm
July–Aug., Fri. and Sat: 10am to 6pm

Tartan Hill Winery

Go from Fenn Valley Winery to Tartan Hill Winery. Take M-31 North to New Era Exit /Stony Lake Road. Go west 1 1/2 miles to 52nd Ave. and turn right on the dirt road for a quarter of a mile.

This wine tasting room is small and rustic. I can imagine riding to it in the 1890s and tieing my horse to a hitching post. The winery is surrounded by their vines with over-looming foliage that sways from the lake's breath.

Bob and Mary Cameron own this winery. Bob manages the grapes and is the winemaker, and his wife assists in pouring and talking to the tourists about their wines. Bob, a retired history teacher, had always wanted to do something with his hands. As he succinctly put it, "What could be better than putting a stick in the ground, having grapes grow on it, crushing and fermenting the fruit and then sitting and talking to people all day about it?"

Bob and his family began planting their vines in 1985. They planted all of the vines, including digging the holes and putting in the posts themselves. Tartan has 30 % viniferas and 70% hybrids– the hybrids are excellent. Their labor paid off with their first gold medal for the Tartan Mist that captured the honor at the American Wine Society's commercial winery competition.

The Camerons have traveled extensively throughout Europe sampling many different wines. Bob really enjoys Rhone wine and tries to mirror the taste in his Red Proprietor's Reserve, which has a leathery, tart taste. It takes two years to make, and he uses his '98, '99, and 2000 harvests. This is definitely a must-try during your visit. For the white wine drinker, try the White Proprietor's Reserve. You won't be sorry. This wine has a blend of Vidal, Seyval and Vignoles, with a hint of oak and a buttery flavor, smooth but not sweet. Tartan Hill Winery serves six different wines–each with a distinct taste.

Tartan Hill Winery

4937 S. 52nd Avenue
New Era, MI 49446
(616) 861-4657

Hours:
June 1–Labor Day:
Open daily from Noon to 5pm

Jomagrha Vineyards and Winery

From Tartan Hill Winery head north again for Jomagrha Vineyards and Winery. Take US-31 north to Pentwater and exit at Oceana. Turn left and go over the overpass and turn right on S. Pere Marquette Highway, (Old Hwy 31). Head down this road and the winery is on your left. You can't miss this barn-like structure, with handmade wreaths gracing the exterior. The winery sits between Bass Lake and the highway. Jomagrha was the first commercial winery in Mason County.

John and Mary Sanford own Jomagrha Vineyards and Winery. John, a former hydrographic surveyor for international corporations, worked mostly abroad, while Mary, an editor of the local newspaper, managed the household and raised the kids. By 1991, the Sanfords had had enough of that lifestyle and John wanted to spend more time with his family.

John had always been interested in fermentation, so it was a natural career crossover for him when he decided to become a winemaker and grape grower.

The Jomagrha Winery produced its first wines for the public in 1999. The first harvest was in September of 2000, yielding a variety of hybrids and viniferas.

Sanford tested the limits with his talented winemaking. He likes dry wine and makes an unusual late harvest wine that is dry, tart and floral. This is definitely worth the trip.

The winery's Three Sisters Blush is named after the famous Three Sisters Hills that guard

Bass Lake. You can see the Three Sisters standing tall from the winery. This wine is made mostly with Vidal, which gives it a flowery taste, and Seyval grapes. The estate-grown Cabernet is used to blush it. Sanfords' semi-sweet white, The Old Lady, is a best-seller.

Jomagrha Vineyards and Winery

7365 S. Pere Marquette Hwy.
Pentwater, MI 49449
(616) 869-4236

www.jomagrha.com

Hours:
Open April 13th–Oct 1st
Wed.–Sun: 1pm to 6pm

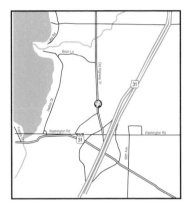

Southwest Michigan

Tourism Information

Michigan Travel Bureaus, Associations and Chambers of Commerce

Web Site: http://mel.lib.mi.us/michigan/recreation/orgs.html

Harbor Country Chamber of Commerce

530 South Whittaker Street Suite F
New Buffalo, MI 49117
Phone: (616) 469-5409
Fax: (616) 469-2257

Web Site: www.harborcountry.org/

Grand Rapids Chamber of Commerce

111 Pearl Street NW
Grand Rapids, MI 49503
Phone: (616) 771-0300
Fax: (616) 771-0318

Web Site: www.grandrapids.org

Inns, Bed & Breakfasts, Cottages and Camping

Saint Joseph Riverwatch Inn

711 West Main Street
Benton Harbor, MI 49022
Phone: (616) 926-8818
Fax: (616) 926-0159

Warren Dunes State Park Campgrounds

Red Arrow Highway
Sawyer, MI
Phone: (616) 426-4013

Kingsley House

626 West Main Street
Fennville, MI 49408
Phone: (616) 561-6425

Inn at Union Pier

9708 Berrien Street
Union Pier, MI 49129
Phone: (616) 469-4700

Chestnut House Bed and Breakfast

1911 Lakeshore Drive
Saint Joseph, MI 49085-1667
Phone: (616) 983-7413
Fax: (616) 983-2122

The Pebble House

15093 Lakeshore Road
Lakeside, MI 49116
Phone: (616) 469-1416

Riverbend Retreat

Saint Joseph Township
254 Jakway Street
Benton Harbor, MI 49022
Phone: (616) 926-2220
Fax: (509) 357-2847

Contact: Patricia A. Jordan

White Rabbit Inn Bed and Breakfast

14634 Red Arrow Highway
Lakeside, MI 49116-0725
Phone: (800) 967-2224
Fax: (616) 469-5843

Rivers Edge Bed and Breakfast

9902 Community Hall Road
Union Pier, MI 49129
Phone: (616) 469-6860

South Cliff Inn Bed and Breakfast

1900 Lakeshore Drive
Saint Joseph, MI 49085
Phone: (616) 983-4881
Fax: (616) 983-7391

Lake Michigan Beach Cottage

2311 South State Street
Saint Joseph, MI 49085
Phone: (616) 983-1328

Lakeview Cottage

2809 West Bundy Road
Coloma, MI 49038
Phone: (616) 849-1329

Nancy's Lakeview Rentals

801 Lions Park Drive
Saint Joseph, MI 49085
Phone: (616) 982-0075
Fax: (616) 982-1153

Contact: Nancy and Al Vredberg

Sans Souci Euro Inn and Cottages
19265 South Lakeside Road
New Buffalo, MI 49117
Phone: (616) 756-3141
Fax: (616) 756-3141

Arts and Entertainment

Berrien County Historical Courthouse
Berrien County Historical Association
313 North Cass Street
Berrien Springs, MI 49103
Phone: (616) 471-1202

Old-style courthouse, blacksmith, jail-house and the oldest two-story log cabin in the state.

Curious Kids' Museum
415 Lake Boulevard
Saint Joseph, MI 49085
Phone: (616) 983-CKID

Krasl Art Center
707 Lake Boulevard
Saint Joseph, MI 49085
Phone: (616) 983-0271

Several galleries and a library–lectures and classes offered.

Hillside Orchards
8198 Fleisher Lane
Berrien Springs, MI 49103
Phone: (616) 471-7558

Enjoy fresh apples, peaches, nectarines and many other fruits.

Sunrise Farms
1280 Hillandale Road
Benton Harbor, MI 49022
Phone: (616) 944-1457

Enjoy ciders, pickles, blueberries and red raspberries, along with many other fruits and vegetables.

Oronoko Lakes Campground
1788 East Snow Road
Berrien Springs, MI 49103
Phone: (616) 471-7389

This is an ideal location for bass fishing, especially if you have children.

Lake Michigan Hills Golf Club
2520 Kerlikowske Road
Benton Harbor, MI 49022
Phone: (616) 849-3266
(800) BIRDIES

Niles Canoe Rental
1520 North Business 31
Niles, MI 49120
Phone: (616) 683-5110
Contact: Matt Meersman

Tubing, canoeing and kayaking on the only natural whitewater in southwest Michigan.

Czar's 505
505 Pleasant Street Suite 303
Saint Joseph, MI 49085
Phone: (616) 983-4111

Featuring comedy and musical acts.

Mendel Center for Arts and Technology
2755 East Napier Avenue
Benton Harbor, MI 49022
Phone: (616) 927-1221
(800) 252-1LMC

Theatre features plays and musicals, and serves as a convention center.

Southwestern Michigan Symphony Orchestra
513 Ship Street
Saint Joseph, MI 49085
Phone: (616) 982-4030

Contact: Adrian J. Reimers

Fernwood Botanic Garden and Nature Center
13988 Range Line Road
Niles, MI 49120
Phone: (616) 683-8653 or (616) 695-6491

105 acres of absolutely stunning natural beauty. They also offer educational classes and programs.

Shopping

Gallery on the Alley
611 Broad Street
Saint Joseph, MI 49085
Phone: (616) 983-6261

Contact: Vicky Nemethy

Arts and crafts by American artists.

The Orchards Mall
1800 Pipestone Road
Benton Harbor, MI 49022
Phone: (616) 927-4467

Over 60 stores.

Restaurants

Bill Knapp's
848 Ferguson Road
Benton Harbor, MI 49022
Phone: (616) 925-3212
(800) 968-9611

Casual family restaurant.

Lighthouse Depot Brewpub and Restaurant
1 Lighthouse Lane
Saint Joseph, MI 49085
Phone: (616) 98-BREWS

Grande Mere Inn
5800 Red Arrow Highway
Stevensville, MI 49127
Phone: (616) 429-3591

Bistro on the Boulevard
521 Lake Boulevard
Saint Joseph, MI 49085
Phone: (616) 983-3882

Fine French cuisine.

Mark III
4179 M-139
Saint Joseph, MI 49085
Phone: (616) 429-2941

Mexican and American cuisine.

Tosi's
4337 Ridge Road
Stevensville, MI 49127
Phone: (616) 429-3689
(800) 218-7745

Italian cuisine.

Santaniello's Restaurant and Pizzeria
2262 West Glenlord Road
Stevensville, MI 49127
Phone: (616) 429-3966

Contact: Margaret, Kerri or Rolf
Italian cuisine with a generous
vegetarian menu.

Schu's Grill and Bar
501 Pleasant Street
Saint Joseph, MI 49085
Phone: (616) 983-7248

Casual restaurant with a beautiful view
of Lake Michigan.

For more information on attractions
in Southwest Michigan, please go to
www.swmichigan.org

Bowers Harbor Vineyards

57

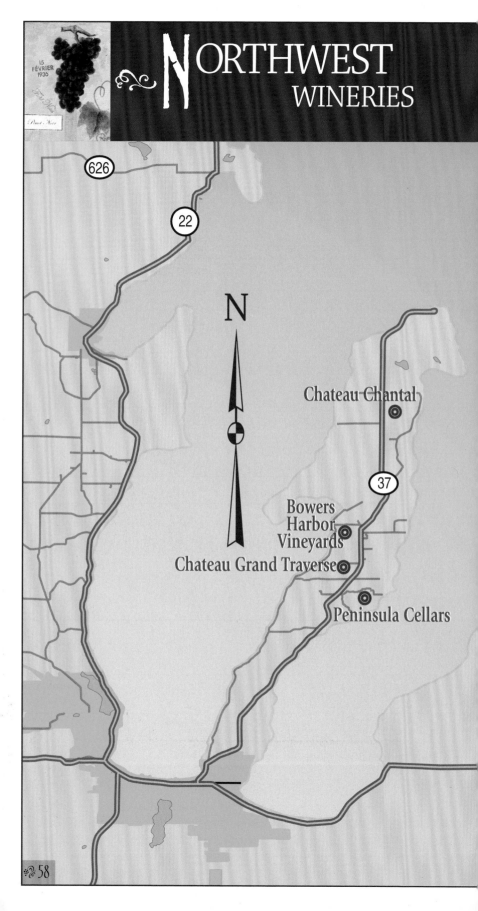

626

22

N

Chateau Chantal

37

Bowers
Harbor
Vineyards

Chateau Grand Traverse

Peninsula Cellars

TOUR 3

Northwest Region

The Old Mission Peninsula and Leelanau
Peninsula are two of the four federally approved
American Viticultural Areas in Michigan. The
northernmost of Michigan's wine regions is located on the 45th parallel, the same latitude as the
great European regions of Bordeaux and Chianti.
Northern Michigan has the optimum microclimate for many grape varieties such as Pinot
Grigio (also known as Pinot Gris), Chardonnay
and optimum sparkling wine varieties. There are
13 wineries that we have listed in this area. They
are close together to offer any traveler a great
weekend getaway. So relax, have fun, and
enjoy the wine.

Tour 3 — Peninsula Cellars

Cheryl Rogers

Peninsula Cellars

We started from Traverse City on US-31/M-37 heading north. When you get to the end of US-31 at the bay, turn right on M-37. The first winery is Peninsula Cellars. Look for the old schoolhouse.

In 1994, Dave and Joan Kroupa planted seven acres of wine grapes among their 250 acres of fruit orchards. Thus began their journey into winemaking–but it should not be a surprise that this winery also produces cherry and apple wines from the fruit in their orchards.

This winery is housed in an old 19th century schoolhouse. The Kroupas have done everything to keep that historic ambience alive, from the hardwood floors to the original windows, to the blackboards.

As cute as the schoolhouse is, it is the wine that is the attention grabber. In 1998, Bryan Ulbrich came aboard as winemaker. He has been very successful at penetrating the old Peninsula with the winery's wine, and thus placing Peninsula Cellars on the map as a premier wine producer in the region. The 1999 Select Riesling has a very good balance with a dense lime flavor. This is a serious wine. Peninsula Cellars has five different vineyards just for Rieslings. There is also the 1999 Gewürztraminer, a full-bodied white wine with floral aromas that one cannot mistake for anything other than a Gewürztraminer. This is a must-try. Peninsula Cellars Winery is known for its white wines, so I also must mention their 2000 Pinot Blanc, a crisp apple and lush pear-like white wine that is delicious.

Peninsula Cellars

11480 Center Rd. (M-37)
Traverse City, MI 49686
Phone: (231) 933-9787

www.peninsulacellars.com

Hours:
May–Oct., Mon–Sat: 10am to 6pm
Sun: Noon to 6pm
Nov–April, Sat. & Sun: Noon to 5pm

Chateau Grand Traverse Winery and Vineyards

From Peninsula Cellars head straight north to Chateau Grand Traverse on M-37. Go several miles up the road and turn left on Center Road. Watch for signs.

Pomegranate and eggplant hues reflect off the foliage and capture your attention the moment you arrive at Chateau Grand Traverse. Founded in 1974 by Edward O'Keefe, Sr., his sons now oversee this vast estate. Edward Sr. got his first taste of wine in 1953 while stationed in Paris, France during the Korean War. He liked the terrain and climate of Northern Michigan and purchased breathtaking rolling hills that overlook Grand Traverse Bay. He hired earth movers to contour the side of a hill in order for the vines to get more of a south-western exposure and better drainage without pockets for snow and water to gather.

The Chateau Grand Traverse focus is on six key European viniferas such as Johannisburg Riesling, Chardonnay, Gamay Noir, Merlot, Pinot Noir and Cabernet Franc. The vineyard is 100% viniferas which grow steadily on Old Peninsula because of the surrounding bays. The winery produces approximately 20,000 cases annually from their estate, and every year they sell out.

The winery and vineyards are beautifully set up to accommodate tourists and locals.

Most of the wine made there is estate wine. Some of the wine juice is obtained from other wineries on Old Peninsula. Try their 1998 Reserve Riesling with a definite aroma of apples, pears and a touch of almond, or the 1999 Dry Riesling, a crisp and musky lime-like wine. For a semi-dry Riesling try the 1999, a soft and smooth wine which lingers nicely.

The 1998 Chardonnay, a gold medal winner, has delightful fruit flavors of fig and melon and the buttery, toasty oak in the finish that barrel fermentation can give to a white wine. Look for their 1999 Late Harvest Johannesburg Riesling, a wine with a good balance of sweetness and acidity that is hard to come by. Other must-tries are the 1998 Gamay Noir and the 1998 Merlot, both of which are aged in French-American oak.

While on the Old Mission Peninsula, try to stay at The Inn at Chateau Grand Traverse. The Inn only has 6 guest rooms but is very elegant and spacious. Each room has a balcony and most have panoramic views of Grand Traverse Bay. All rooms are equipped with modern amenities. During the summer months it is quite busy and you have to make your reservations way ahead of time. High season, rooms are $150.00 a night; in the off season they are considerably cheaper.

Chateau Grand Traverse

12239 Center Road
Traverse City, MI 49686
Winery Phone: (231) 223-7355
The Inn: (231) 223-9484 or (800) 283-0247
Fax: (231) 223-4105

Call for information about their three tasting rooms around Traverse City.

www.cgtwines.com

Summer Hours:
Mon.–Sat: 10am to 7pm
Sun: Noon to 6pm
Fall tours available

Bowers Harbor Vineyards

Go back to M-37 north one mile to Bowers Harbor Road and make a left turn. This is a very sharp, almost hairpin turn. I missed the sign twice–so go slowly. Follow the winding road for 1/2 mile and you will see the signs.

This entire winery, on over 40 acres, overlooks Bowers Harbor. It is quaint and personable and is surrounded by their vineyards, which you drive through to get to the wine tasting room. It is owned by the Stegenga family and is tourist-friendly. The unique mother and son team, Linda and Spencer, are well-informed on the terrain and wines of Michigan.

This land was used as a quarter horse breeding and boarding farm before the Stegenga family purchased it in 1983, and two years later turned the horse barn into a winery. Their first harvest was in 1994–from their vineyard. Today they grow viniferas such as Chardonnay, Pinot Grigio, Riesling, Gewürztraminer, Pinot Noir, Merlot, and Cabernet Franc.

The winery has a unique gift shop. The items move beyond traditional T-shirts to include unique linens with hand-painted winegrapes. Spencer, the manager, oversees the vineyards and wine production. Linda runs the tasting room and is the CFO of the business. Spencer is young and full of charismatic energy. If you have a chance to meet him in the tasting

room, do so, because his enthusiasm for Michigan wines is catching.

Bowers Harbor wines are pleasing and perfect for everyday enjoyment as well as for celebrations. Spencer relies on intuition and hard work to give their winery the best possible reputation. "I like to do everything that I can myself...my expectations are high and I know that only I can get it done the way I want it done." When you drive up to the winery, you will see that love and care in their flourishing vineyards.

For a must-try, the estate unwooded Chardonnay has been aged Sur-Lie in stainless steel. It's a clean and crisp dry wine. There is the 1999 Pinot Grigio, a more floral wine with melon tones. The 1999 Riesling Estate Reserve is a semi-dry white with soft green apple, pineapple and melon tones. It's a very popular German-style wine. This Riesling was the winner of a bronze medal at the American Wine Society competition in 2000. For red wine lovers, a must-try is the Bowers Harbor Red–a full-bodied, fruity red table wine that could accompany almost any meal. Last but not least is the sparkling Blanc de Blanc–full of bubbles and properly dry. Just wonderful!

Bowers Harbor Vineyards

2896 Bowers Harbor Road
Traverse City, MI 49686
Phone: (800) 616-7615
or (231) 223-7615

www.bowersharbor.com

Hours:
Mon.–Sat: 11am to 6pm
Sun: Noon to 6pm

Chateau Chantal

Go back to M-37 and head north three miles from Bowers Harbor. Turn right on Rue de Vin and follow the winding road to the Chateau on the top of the hill.

Chateau Chantal is a remarkably beautiful facility both inside and out. No matter where you stand or sit in this winery you will have a panoramic view of both east and west Grand Traverse Bays. When would-be wine tasters enter through two very grand Italianate wooden doors, they are surrounded by large bay windows which capture the stunning views. The interior is purely unique for Michigan and perhaps even the U.S. I can only describe the winery as elegant beyond words, with warm touches to make one feel relaxed and wish it were their home. Tapestries hang from the walls, and over-stuffed furniture beckons near the stone fireplace. A baby grand piano awaits the player in dignity. All is very majestic.

Chateau Chantal sits on 65 acres of rolling hilltops which straddle a ridge near the northern end of Old Mission Peninsula, making it both the ideal terrain and microclimate for growing the best quality wine grapes.

Chateau Chantal was originally founded by Robert and Nadine Begin in 1983. As they expanded their facility to state-of-the-art, they formed a company and sold off some of the property. Chateau Chantal owns roughly 40 acres of grapevines which produce at least 100 tons of Chardonnay, Riesling, Pinot Noir, Gewürztraminer, Merlot and Cabernet Franc, as well as Pinot Meunier for blending Methode Champenoise. Nearly all of the wine production is done in-house.

The best part of a Chateau Chantal tour is the wine! Winemaker Mark Johnson is one of the few Americans to graduate as an enologist from the renowned school of viticulture at Geisenheim, Polytechnique Wiesbaden. Not only does he make excellent wine, he teaches wine seminars at the Chateau as well. Moreover, if you take a tour of the facility, you will be able to spot one or two interns from renowned European wineries working there to learn more about how to make wine in a modern facility.

Chateau Chantal's premium wines have won many awards. A few on my list of favorites are the 1998 Proprietor's Reserve Chardonnay which won the Best of Show–White Wine award at the 1999 Michigan State Fair. Try the Carpe Diem!, a gold medal-winning sparkling wine made of Chardonnay and a splash of Pinot Noir. Another white to definitely taste is the 1999 Proprietor's Reserve Chardonnay, barrel fermented in new French oak to give it its smoky aroma. It is also a gold medal-winner. For fun, have the Naughty and Nice Reds. Naughty is a dry red and Nice is a semi-sweet blend.

Try to stay at their inn which is right in the winery. There are two suites and one queen-size room and breakfast is served right in the tasting room with a full view of the east bay. They often book up two years in advance, but you can always get in during the off-season.

Chateau Chantal

15900 Rue de Vin
Traverse City, MI 49686
(800) 969-4009
(231) 223-4110

www.chateauchantal.com

Hours:
Open all year–Sundays, Noon to 5pm
Summer, Mon.–Sat: 11am to 9pm
Fall, Mon.–Sat: 11am to 7pm
Winter, Mon.–Sat: 11am to 5pm

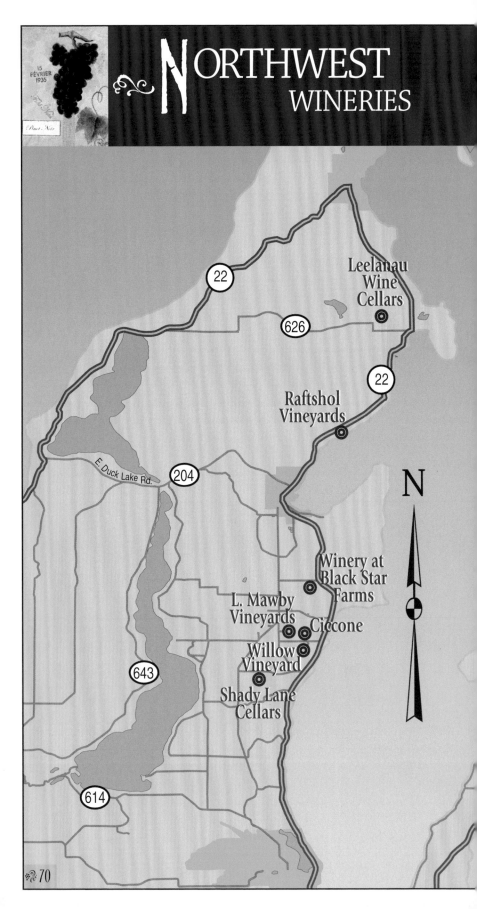

22

Leelanau
Wine
Cellars

626

22

Raftshol
Vineyards

E. Duck Lake Rd. 204

N

Winery at
Black Star
Farms

L. Mawby
Vineyards
Ciccone

Willow
Vineyard

643

Shady Lane
Cellars

614

TOUR 4
Northwest Region

Tour 4 — *Shady Lane Cellars*

Shady Lane Cellars

S tart this tour at Traverse City and take M-22 north seven miles to Shady Lane. Turn left on Shady Lane and drive approximately one mile until you see the winery on your left. You can't miss it.

Shady Lane is located on Leelanau Peninsula. It's a small, handsome boutique winery that resides on a 150-acre farm, strategically located for the mesoclimate created by Lake Michigan and Grand Traverse Bay. This tasting room was once a chicken coop, and luckily the proprietors have left some of the historic reminders such as the small windows on the second floor. The interior's wood beams and stone walls–including a stone fireplace–are surrounded by an Italian tile floor. The tasting bar has a modern, cozy feel.

Owners Joe O'Donnell and Bill Stouten set the winery in motion in 1989, but winemaker Adam Satchwell and sales manager Debra Varnum manage the day-to-day business. Shady Lane Cellars is known for its quality still wines and sparkling wines. Currently they grow 10,000 vines of Chardonnay, Riesling, Vignoles and Pinot Noir, producing some of the top wines on the peninsula.

Some must-tries are the two-time gold medal-winner, 1997 Sparkling Riesling; a bottle-fermented Brut. Excellent! We had this with our Easter dinner and everyone raved about it. The gold medal-winning 1999 Semi-Dry Riesling has a classic apple fruit aroma with a dry and crisp finish. For red wine lovers, the Pinot Noir–with subtle hints of cherry and a soft finish–is not to be missed.

Shady Lane Cellars

9580 Shady Lane
Suttons Bay, MI 49682
Phone: (231) 947-8865

www.shadylanecellars.com

Hours:
May–Oct: Noon to 6pm daily
Or call for appointment.

Ciccone Vineyard and Winery

From Shady Lane turn right out of the driveway and go back toward M-22. Watch for the big red barn and turn left on Elm Valley, then watch for Hill Top Road and turn right. Look for the winery on your left.

All of Ciccone's wines are estate wines, with the exception of Cherricetto, which is part cherry wine and part estate Dolcetto wine. All harvesting and winemaking are done by hand by the Ciccone family. (He refers to his employees and associate wine consultants as family.)

When we arrived, we had to go out into the vineyard to get Mr. Ciccone. He was carefully tending to the vines along with two "family members." Ciccone Winery is the newest in the area and already has a reputation for excellent Cabernet Franc. Silvio Tony Ciccone and Joan Clare Ciccone are the proprietors. It's especially well-known on the peninsula that Tony Ciccone is the father of pop artist Madonna. They even look alike.

The winery is brand new and tourist-friendly. The Ciccones, along with Jon Wakeman, the architect, designed and put the finishing touches on the interior. It is a cross between an Italian village church with high, hand-carved wood beams — and a village saloon, with the wall mirrors and large wine tasting bar. This winery is in good taste and it is not to be missed. Tony is personable and loves to talk about his wine.

The must-tries on my list are the 1999 Gewürztraminer, which has a wonderful peach aroma with a hint of grapefruit. This wine is dry and crisp. For another white wine to sample, the Chardonnay has a spicy fragrance and a touch of oak with a smooth aftertaste. For red wine lovers, try the 1999 Cabernet Franc, a full-bodied red with extra aging and aromas of green pepper and raspberries. The 1999 Dolcetto alone is worth your trip!

Ciccone Vineyard and Winery

10343 E. Hilltop Rd.
Suttons Bay, MI 49682
Phone: (231) 271-5551
Fax: (231) 271-5552

www.cicconevineyards.com

Hours:
April–Nov., Thur.–Sun: Noon to 6pm
Dec.–Mar. by appointment only

L. Mawby Winery

T urn right out of Ciccone Winery and go back to Elm Valley Road. Go right and watch for the L. Mawby Winery sign and address and you will see the vineyard on the right. Turn in the dirt driveway, go past the vineyards and the tasting room is in the back.

L. Mawby Winery has been around since 1978. Larry Mawby, owner and winemaker, is considered one of the gurus on the peninsula. His sparkling wines are said to be some of the best in Michigan. All of Mawby's sparkling wines are produced using Methode Champenoise and all age for up to three years or more in the bottle before release for sale. Mawby's current annual production is around 2,500 cases. Each of his labels has a poem which personifies the wine.

Talisman Brut is an estate blend of Chardonnay, Pinot Noir, Pinot Gris and Vignoles. This Brut is creamy and delicate, but dry. Blanc de Blanc is a sparkling wine produced from 100 percent Chardonnay grapes grown on the Leelanau Peninsula. The Cremant is a rich, full-fruited estate Vignoles wine. Larry claims the 1995 Mille is his best sparkling ever. A limited selection of still wines is also available, including the Vignoles, a crisp, dry white or the Sandpiper, an off-dry white.

Larry Mawby has summer picnics that are the rave on Leelanau Peninsula. They are catered first-class afternoon and evening events featuring, what else? Mawby wine. Tickets can be purchased online and must be obtained in advance.

L. Mawby Winery

4519 S. Elm Valley Rd.
Suttons Bay, MI 49682
Phone: (231) 271-3522
Fax: (231) 271-2927

www.lmawby.com

Hours:
May–Oct: Thurs.–Sun: 1pm to 6pm
Nov. - Apr: Sat. 1pm to 5pm
Or call for appointment

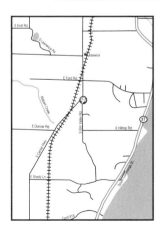

Black Star Farms

From L. Mawby turn right and go up Center Road (633 N) to Revold Road. Turn right and go one mile, and Black Star Farms will be on your right. Entering between the stone pillars you will see the newly planted vineyards terraced on your right. Continue past the Bed & Breakfast Inn, boarding stables and barns and the new winery tasting room is on the right.

This winery is undoubtedly the most beautiful on Leelanau Peninsula. It is grand and a perfect destination for a

weekend retreat. It includes a beautiful inn with seven luxurious guest rooms and an indoor pool!

Lee Lutes is the winemaker and oversees the winery. He is among the younger generation of winemakers who are more willing to take chances, and he has endless energy. Lee helped set up Peninsula Cellars and now he is making his mark at Black Star Farms.

Black Star Farms grows viniferas including Riesling, Chardonnay, Merlot and Cabernet

Franc, Pinot Blanc and Pinot Gris. You can view the wine- and cheese-making processes through the large tasting room windows.

Their red wines are definitely worth buy-ing. The Pinot Noir is outstanding. It's an intense, rich, full-bod-ied red wine. Also try the Cabernet Franc, a wine well worth your visit. It has an earthy and berry fruit aroma. Buy a bottle and have it with your friends when you return home. They will thank you.

For white wines, compare the Chardonnays–one barrel-aged, the other Sur-Lie style–or try the Leorie Riesling, a light semi-dry white with a floral aroma. Black Star has a new distillery for their brandies.

Also visit their tasting room in Paw Paw, Michigan.

Black Star Farms

10844 East Revold Road
Suttons Bay, MI 49682
Phone: (231) 271-4970
Fax: (231) 271-4883

www.blackstarfarms.com

Hours:
Mon.–Fri: 11am to 6pm
Sun: Noon to 6
Open year-round

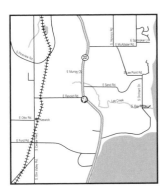

Raftshol Vineyards

Head back to M-22 towards Suttons Bay. Go through Suttons Bay about 2 1/2 miles north and on your right is the winery. You will see the sign. Turn in at the sign and go toward the back. There is a small wine tasting room.

This land was once a dairy farm, then cherry orchard that was owned by Warren and Curtis Raftshol's grandmother in the early 1900s. The brothers inherited the land from their mother, Jean Raftshol. In honor of this gift, they put a striking picture of her at age 20 on all their wine labels.

Since the 1980s the Raftshols have been growing wine grapes. Theirs was the first commercial vineyard in the area to grow red vinifera grapes. Raftshol Red was one of the first red wines made in northern Michigan, and is among the best-known on the peninsula.

The wine list is short but heavy on quality. A must-try is the 1999 Claret, a blend of Cabernet Franc, Cabernet Sauvignon and Merlot. It's full-bodied and delicious. Also try the 1999 Cabernet Sauvignon, also full-bodied, and rich with berry and anise aromas. For white wine lovers, try the 1998 Chardonnay–it's medium-bodied, with aromas of tropical fruit and vanilla.

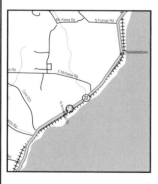

Raftshol Vineyards

1865 N. West Bay Shore Drive
Suttons Bay, MI 49682
Tel/Fax: (231) 271-5650

www.raftsholvineyards.com

Hours:
Daily, Noon to 5pm
Open year-round

Leelanau Wine Cellars

Go back to M-22 and head north to the village of Omena. Look for the country store and take a sharp left 1/4 mile up the hill and the winery is on the right.

This country boutique winery celebrated its 25th anniversary in 2000. Father and son owners Michael and Bob Jacobson started by producing wine from locally grown fruit and grapes. Today they grow vinifera grapes such as Chardonnay, Merlot, and Pinot Noir. Bill Skolnik, renowned for his award-winning wines in Michigan and New York, is the winemaker and vineyard manager.

A must-try is the 1999 Grand Reserve, a barrel-fermented estate Chardonnay, or sample the semi-dry Late Harvest Riesling. The Leelanau Cellars' Tall Ship Chardonnay has won several gold medals. It is a blend of estate-grown and locally purchased grapes and is barrel fermented. Their pear nectar is a unique blend of Californian pear brandy and fresh pear juice from the region.

While you are tasting their delicious wines take a good look at their labels. They are beautiful! And if you walk up the hill to the vineyard, you'll be rewarded with a striking view of Grand Traverse Bay.

Leelanau Wine Cellars

12683 E. Tatch Rd
Omena, MI 49674
Phone: (231) 386-5201

Summer Hours:
Mon–Sun: 11am to 6pm
Open 7 days a week year-round
Call first in the off-season.

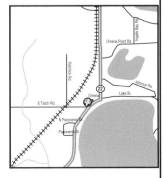

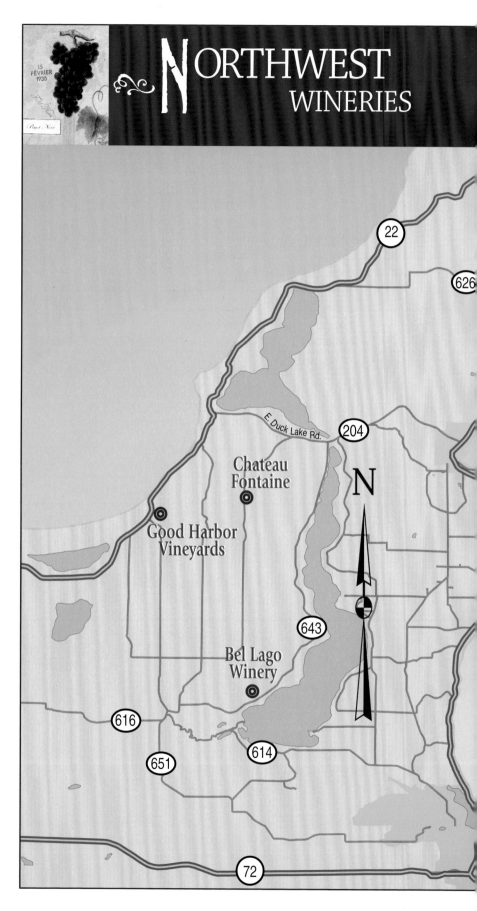

15
FÉVRIER
1935

Pinot Noir

22

626

E. Duck Lake Rd.

204

Chateau
Fontaine

Good Harbor
Vineyards

N

643

Bel Lago
Winery

616

651

614

72

Chateau

Fontaine

WINE TASTING
AND SALES

TOUR 5
Northwest Region

Good Harbor Vineyards

On the Leelanau Peninsula, take M-22 to M-204 and head west back to M-22. Turn left three miles south of Leland and look for Bibbs Farm Market. The winery is right behind it. You will see the signs.

The drive to Good Harbor is very scenic and lined with hidden bakeries, boutiques and

antique shops along the way. This winery is simple with simply good wine. It is owned by Bruce and Debbie Simpson, and Bruce is the winemaker. They have a 450-acre multi-fruit farm that includes 50 acres of wine grapes.

Bruce likes to make wine and have people enjoy what he produces. In fact, he hires local artists to create fun-loving labels to go with his philosophy that wine should add joy to life. If you get a chance to speak with him in the tasting room, do so.

On the must-try list is Good Harbor's Pinot Gris Reserve, a gold winner at the Michigan State Fair in 1999. This reserve is a barrel-fer-

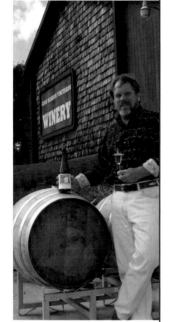

mented dry wine with nice, tropical fruit and toasty butterscotch flavors. The White Riesling is a perfect wine with any fowl or even Chinese food. It is crisp and aromatic. The 1999 Riesling won a gold at the Great Lakes Wine Competition. For a Chardonnay try the Vintners Reserve–wonderfully fruity with a clean bite. Good Harbor makes a great sparkling wine, Moonstruck, which is a Brut with good bubbles and tanginess.

Good Harbor Vineyards

34 S. Manitou Trail
Lake Leelanau, MI 49653
Phone: (231) 256-7165

www.goodharbor.com

Hours:
May 20–Oct.31,
Mon.–Sat: 11am to 5pm
Sun: Noon to 5pm
Winter months the winery is open
Sat.–Sun., 12pm to 5pm.
Nov.–Dec.,
Saturdays, Noon to 5pm
Jan.–May 20, call for appointment

Chateau Fontaine

Go left out of the driveway of Good Harbor to M-22. Go right to Shomberg Drive and turn right. Go to Dufek Road and turn left. Drive through the woods to French Road and turn right. Go past the dairy farm and look for the sign on the right.

This is a brand new winery in Michigan and it is ready for tourists. It is clean and spacious and embedded in the woods. Grape-themed totem poles stand guard at the entrance. Surrounding this winery are rolling hills of vineyards full of Pinot Gris, Chardonnay and Riesling. Don't forget to stop at this new winery, and try the Riesling! There's also a new off-site tasting room.

Chateau Fontaine

2290 South French Road
Lake Leelanau, MI 49653
(231) 256-0000

Hours:
May, Open Sat–Sun:
Noon to 5pm

June–Oct: Open Wed–Sun.
Nov–Jan: Open Weekends

Call ahead for hours or to make an appointment.

Bel Lago

From Chateau Fontaine's driveway turn right on French Road to Kabot and turn right. Right again on Lake Shore Drive, then watch for the sign.

Charles Edson and Amy Lezzoni are both acclaimed horticulturists at Michigan State University and are the owners of Bel Lago. The winery is surrounded by their 30+ acres of vineyards and overlooks Lake Leelanau. They have tiled their wine tasting bar in the aquamarine hues of the lakes.

Winemaker Bob Sarniak runs the winery full-time as well as oversees the vineyards' Pinot Gris, Chardonnay, Cayuga, Riesling, Gewürztraminer and Muscats, and a few reds including Pinot Noir, Pinot Munier, Cab Franc, and Merlot.

Bob makes an award-winning sparkling wine, Bel Lago Brut, and a mean red, Tempesta, blended of Cabernet Franc and Merlot. This wine usually sells out every year. Bel Lago also makes an off-dry wine, Primavera, made from estate Gewürztraminer, Muscat, Cayuga and Seyval.

Bel Lago Winery

6530 S. Lake Shore Drive
Cedar , MI 49651
(231) 228-4800
Fax (231) 228-4888

Hours:
May–Nov., Thurs.–Mon:
Noon to 5pm
Call ahead for hours during the off-season.

Northwest Michigan

Tourism Information

Michigan Travel Bureaus, Associations and Chambers of Commerce

Web Site: http://mel.lib.mi.us/michigan/recreation/orgs.html

Traverse City Chamber of Commerce
202 East Grandview Parkway
Traverse City, MI 49684
Phone: (231) 947-5075
Fax: (231) 946-2565

Web Site: www.tcchamber.org

Petoskey Chamber of Commerce
401 East Mitchell Street
Petoskey, MI 49770
Phone: (231) 347-4150
Fax: (231) 348-1810

Web Site: www.petoskey.com/

Inns, Bed & Breakfasts, Cottages and Camping

Campbell's Leelanau Beachfront Rentals
4516 Cherokee Lane
Bloomfield Hills, MI 48301
Phone: (810) 626-0844

A Place in Thyme Bed and Breakfast
13140 Isthmus Street
Omena, MI 49674
Phone: (231) 386-7006

Baypointe Resort
6574 NW Bay Shore Drive
Northport, MI 49670
Phone: (800) 700-5491

Northport Bay Retreat
6512 West Bay Shore Drive
Northport, MI 49670
Phone: (231) 935-0111
Fax: (231) 941-2334

Sleepy Bear Campground
6760 West Empire Highway M-72
Empire, MI 49630
Phone: (231) 326-5566

Fax: (231) 326-5711

Contact: Ray and Mary Savage

Grey Hare Inn
West Rue de Carroll
P.O. Box 1535
Traverse City, MI 49686
Phone: (231) 947-2214
(800) 873-0652

Contact: Cindy and Jay Ruzak

Falling Waters Lodge
200 West Cedar
Leland, MI 49654
Phone: (616) 256-9832

Whaleback Inn
P.O. Box 1125
Leland, MI 49654
Phone: (616) 256-9090

Neahtawanta Inn
1308 Neahtawanta Road
Traverse City, MI 49686
Phone: (231) 223-7315

Cider House Bed and Breakfast
5515 Barney Road
Traverse City, MI 49686
Phone: (231) 947-2833
Fax: (231) 947-2833

The Grainery
2951 Hartman Road
Traverse City, MI 49684
Phone: (231) 946-8325

Contact: Ron and Julie Kucera

Whispering Waters Bed and Breakfast Retreat
2020 Sarns Road
Traverse City, MI 49686
Phone: (231) 941-5557
(888) 880-5557
Fax: (231) 941-0321

The Old Mill Pond Inn
202 West 3rd Street
Northport, MI 49670
Phone: (231) 386-7341

Contact: David Chropak

Omena Sunset Lodge Bed and Breakfast
12819 Tatch Road
Northport, MI 49674
Phone: (231) 386-7313

Centennial Inn
7251 East Alpers Road
Lake Leelanau, MI 49653-9629
Phone: (231) 271-6460

Frieda's Bed and Breakfast
3141 Omena Point Road
Omena, MI 49674
Phone: Summer: 231/386-7274
Winter: (210) 659-4041
(closed for winter)

Contact: Frieda Putnam

Arts & Entertainment

Sleeping Bear Dunes National Lakeshore
9922 Front Street
Empire, MI 49630-9797
Phone: (231) 326-5134
Fax: (231) 326-5382

Web Site: www.nps.gov/slbe/

This 35-mile stretch of natural beauty offers boating, fishing, snorkeling, snow-shoeing, cross-country skiing, dune climbing and much more.

Manitou Islands

Located in the Sleeping Bear Dunes National Lakeshore, these islands are home to 100-foot tall cedars, a ship-wreck, a historic lighthouse, rare wild-flowers, and camping areas.

Interlochen Center for the Arts
P.O. Box 199
Interlochen, MI 49643
Phone: (231) 276-7200

School of arts, presenting both profes-sional and student productions.

Turtle Creek Casino
7741 Michigan Highway 72
Williamsburg, MI 49690
Phone: (231) 267-9574
(888) 777-8946

Shimmer's Nightclub
Holiday Inn
615 East Front Street
Traverse City, MI 49686
Phone: (231) 947-3700

Top 40 dance hits played by live bands and DJ's.

Border's Books and Music
2612 Crossing Circle
Traverse City, MI 49686
Phone: (231) 933-0412

Live music in the café several times each week.

The Other Place Comedy Club
738 South Garfield Street
Traverse City, MI 49686
Phone: (231) 941-0988

Two different show times every Friday and Saturday night.

Con Foster Historical Museum
Clinch Park
Cass Street and Grandview Parkway
Traverse City, MI 49686
Phone: (231) 922-4905

Michigan Native American and Pioneer heritage.

Bay Meadows Golf Course
5220 Barney Road
Traverse City, MI 49686
Phone: (231) 946-7927

Golfing for all skill levels.

Shopping

Grand Traverse Mall
U.S. Highway 31 and
South Airport Road
Traverse City, MI 49686
Phone: (231) 922-0077

Downtown Traverse City
Front and Union Streets
Phone: (231) 922-2050

Many unique shops in a cozy hometown environment.

**Grand Traverse Resort
Tower-Gallery of Shops**
6300 U.S. 31 North
Acme, MI 49610
Phone: (231) 938-2100

High-end, unique shopping.

Antique Company East Bay
4386 U.S. Highway 31 North
Traverse City, MI 49686
Phone: (231) 938-3000

Leelanau Cheese Company
5042 West Bay Shore Drive
Omena, MI 49674
Phone: (231) 386-7731

Peddler's Corner
119 South Union Street
Traverse City, MI 49686
Phone: (231) 947-1198

Thrift-store shopping.

Stewart-Zack's
118 East Front Street
Traverse City, MI 49684
Phone: (231) 947-2322

Specialty home decorations.

Restaurants

Apache Trout Grill
13671 SW Bay Shore Drive
Traverse City, MI 49686
Phone: (231) 947-7079

*Fresh saltwater fish, pasta, steak
and ribs in a casual environment
with a great view of the West
Grand Traverse Bay.*

Boone's Prime Time Pub
102 North Saint Joseph
Suttons Bay, MI 49682
Phone: 231/271-6688

*Family restaurant specializing
in steaks and seafood.*

Hatties
111 North Saint Joseph
Suttons Bay, MI 49682
Phone: (231) 271-6222

*Elegant atmosphere—and menu offers
many of the wines from the area.
Call for reservations.*

Key to the County
P.O. Box 138
Lake Leelanau, MI 49653
Phone: (231) 256-5397

Fine dining.

Boathouse Bluewater Bistro
14039 Peninsula Drive
Traverse City, MI 49686
Phone: (231) 223-4030

*Casual atmosphere with first-rate service
and outstanding cuisine. Specialties
include Madeira duck breast caesar
salad, potato lasagna, sesame tuna and
portobello escargot. On Sundays, brunch
is accompanied by a live jazz band.*

Bowers Harbor Inn
13512 Peninsula Drive
Traverse City, MI 49686
Phone: (231) 223-4222

*Acoustic guitar entertainment on week-
ends. Specialties include crab-stuffed
shrimp, fish in a bag and steak d'Alaska.
Reservations are recommended.*

China Fair
1357 South Airport Road
Traverse City, MI 49684
Phone: (231) 941-5844

*Oriental cuisine including Cantonese,
Szechwan and Thai.*

Grand Traverse Dinner Train
642 Railroad Place
Traverse City, MI 49686
Phone: (231) 933-3768

*Elegant 5-course dinner served on a Pull-
man-style train. Lunch is family-oriented.*

Minerva's
Park Place Hotel
300 East State Street
Traverse City, MI 49684
Phone: (231) 946-5093

Recently renovated restaurant.

*For more information on attractions in
Northwest Michigan, please go to
www.insiders.com/traverse/*